The Voice Between the Lines

A Carnegie Writers Publication
from the Summer 2025 Teen Authors Workshop

Authors & Contributors

Authors

Kerriona Alexander | Raymond Bass, Jr. | Kayah Baxter
Adyen Davis | Madison Dismukes | Justyn Harris
Anijah Hatten | Kadiyah Inmon | Jaliyah Jarrett
Nijah Jones | Je'Corean Lee | Londyn McDonald
Giliam Primero Mejia | Ismaeel Moskinzada | Jaleah Parks
Andrea Reynolds | Dorian Rhodes | Alayna Tucker
Ronnie Turner | Tsurah Waire | Rylan Wetsell

Program Facilitators

Flor Abarca | Kemi Elufiede | Mytecia Myles | Sabrina Wai

Editors

Carissa Barker-Stucky | Kemi Elufiede

The Voice Between the Lines
Published by Carnegie Writers, Inc.

ISBN: 979-8-9923614-2-1 (print)
ISBN: 979-8-9923614-3-8 (ebook)

Contents

Kerriona Alexander

Kerriona Alexander is a creative soul with a passion for cosmetology—especially doing hair and lashes. Whether she's experimenting with new styles or playing in a band, she loves expressing herself through art and beauty. Her favorite color is purple, and she enjoys writing imaginative fiction stories in her free time. Kerriona Alexander's creativity shines in everything she does, from her styling skills to her storytelling.

The Witch's Daughters

Short Story

One dark, cloudy night, a witch finally gave birth to twins in Lincoln Hospital at 12:35. "Waaaa!" the twins cried. The mother decided to name one twin Alisha and the other Ashley. Ten years later, the twins became very disobedient: they wouldn't listen to their mother and would throw things at the other students at Benchware Elementary.

Soon enough, the mother realized it was time…but for what?

When the twins came home, she decided to tell them they have to prepare for war. The girls' excitement took over, and they screamed, "With who, Mother, with *who*?!"

"Against the Polar and Lava twins; we have to fight over the pink, blue, and purple castle that comes with magic and potions."

"Mother, doesn't it mean we need a new name as well?" Alisha asks.

"Yes, you're right," their mother says.

"Woah! What about the Two-Faced Twins, Moon and Sun?"

"Perfect!" Mother says.

The girls train for the next two years; they practices using weapons and learning fighting skills. Then they were ready for war. The Two-Faced Twins and their mother flew through the cloudy, cold sky; once they arrived at the battleground, they prayed and started the war. The Polar and Lava twins began throwing ice and lava, but the Moon and Sun twins jumped and leaped over the ice as well as

trying to dodge the lava. Moon threw stars at Polar, while Sun tried to hit Lava with her own fire. Boom! Sun hit Polar instead, and she fell and screamed out for help– but it was too late, as Lava was distracted. Moon and Sun attacked her together. After they won, the twins lived happily in their new pink, blue, and purple magical castle until they got old.

The End

The Elevator

Playwriting

[Scene 1: Grace's home.]

MOM
Grace! Come Downstairs!

GRACE
[with high-pitched voice]
Yes, Mom?

MOM
You have to come to work with me today.

GRACE
sighs
Do I really have to? I promised Laurn I would come over!

MOM
[firmly]
Grace Green Carter, I will not repeat myself.

GRACE
Yes, ma'am...

MOM:
Make sure you wear your blue shirt.

[End Scene]

[Scene 2: Office lobby]

MOM
Grace, head on up in the elevator and fetch those papers I told you about, please.

GRACE walks towards the elevator.

GRACE
[to self, grumpily]
God help me.

GRACE enters the elevator. While she's waiting, JASON enters. GRACE smiles in greeting as he selects his floor. As the door closes and the elevator starts moving, GRACE speaks.

GRACE
Hi, how are you?

JASON
Hello! I'm good, how about–

There's a loud boom. The elevator stops moving, GRACE and JASON staggering slightly with the abruptness.

GRACE
[Freaking out]
Oh my God, what is happening?!

JASON
[Nervous]
Calm down, let's press the help button.

GRACE
And I'll call my mom; she can probably help...

JASON
Yeah, I will call my dad. Hopefully he answers...he's pretty busy.

They both attempt tol call their parents and get sent to voicemail. No one answers the 'help' button, either. They are left waiting. There

is an awkward silence.

GRACE
So...Do you work here?

JASON
No, my dad does. I'm helping him out.

GRACE
Oh. Well, my mom works here. I was helping, as well.

Another awkward pause.

JASON
How long you think we're going to be here?

GRACE
I hope not forever...

They laugh nervously. The elevator drops suddently. GRACE screams.

GRACE
What is going on?!

JASON
I don't know! I want it to stop!

UNKNOWN VOICE
laughs through the elevator speakers

GRACE
Hello?? Help us, please!

UNKNOWN VOICE
stops laughing
You must complete my challenges!

GRACE
Ok...well, what are the challenges?

UNKNOWN VOICE
You must answer my questions.

JASON
Fine. I'll go first. But what happens if we're wrong?

UNKNOWN VOICE
You will be trapped in here for five extra minutes. First question! How long has this building been standing?

JASON
Oh, I know this! My dad just told me this morning: 12 years.

UNKNOWN VOICE
Correct!

UNKNOWN VOICE cracks slightly, sounding like MOM,

GRACE
[whispering]
Hang on, that sounds like my mom...She was acting pretty weird this morning.

JASON
[also whispering]
Really? So was my dad...

The challenge continues, and the voice changes throughout. Sometimes it is robotic, but sometimes the filter crackles and sounds like MOM or JASON'S DAD. After a few rounds of trivia:

UNKNOWN VOICE
Well done. You have successfully answered all of my questions.

GRACE
Can we leave now?

UNKNOWN VOICE
Sure, but first...

MOM
Sorry, Grace...

JASON'S DAD
Sorry, son.

GRACE
Wait, *what*?! I told you, Jason!

JASON
[stunned]
I can't believe it...

The elevator slows to a stop. JASON and GRACE stare at their parents once the door opens before moving to restrain them until POLICE can arrive.

[End Scene]

Women's Rights

Article Writing, Informal

Why is it important for each new generation to learn about women's rights?

As recently as the 1970s, women had to fight for equality.

Throughout America's history, women did not have the same freedom and decision-making power as men. Women weren't even allowed to vote until August 26, 1920; additionally, rights were granted to white women first. African American women still faced challenges like poll taxes that made it more difficult for them to vote. As women grew tired and frustrated from being treated differently, American writer Elizabeth Cady Stanton stepped up to become an important leader in the fight for women's rights.

Since women didn't have as many rights as men, how did they work?

Women either worked as nannies, cooks, or cleaners for wealthy families or stayed home to perform those tasks for their husbands. Women who didn't have a family and young, unmarried girls often had dangerous factory jobs. They faced long hours, small pay, and dangerous conditions.

Women spent decades, even centuries, being told what they could and could not do. Instead, they should be free to make decisions about their own lives, bodies, and property, without needing anyone else's permission. Women were made to feel like dolls and playthings, bossed around by men and then mocked when they started fighting for more rights. Teaching newer generations this

history helps us understand how far society has come and why it's important to keep pushing forward. In many parts of the world, women are still fighting for rights. Teaching young people about this helps build a future where everyone, no matter their gender, shall be treated equally.

Kayah Baxter

Kayah Baxter is a creative and resilient scholar from Tennessee. She enjoys reading, writing, playing musical instruments, and knitting—activities that help her stay grounded and inspired. Whether painting, drawing, sculpting, or writing, Kayah expresses her true self through art. She plans on becoming a successful orthodontist and is committed to lifelong growth as she works to become the best version of herself.

Season's Change, Some Don't

Poem

Like butterflies,
like open skies,
a puddle left
from softened rain.

An autumn breeze
slips through the trees
and summer's back
again.

Then winter hums,
then quietly goes,
as far
as we may know.

But some cold stays
beneath the skin,
a chill that creeps
and crawls within.

Brightest Star

Short Story

On a cool, early fall morning, my mom and I were walking around a bit outside as we waited for other children to arrive at school.

I had made some kind of joke or remark, one in which I wasn't being serious, but she answered me literally.

"Ugh, I *know*, Mom, I was being 'Star-castic'!"

She paused and turned to look at my completely serious seven-year-old face. She then broke out laughing.

She laughed so hard. Not loud, but it was an incredibly amused, bubbly laugh.

It took a few minutes of my confused giggling and her laughing for her to get to what she was trying to say.

"Did you just say 'Star-castic'? Honey, it's 'Sarcastic'!" she said before she began to laugh again, at which point I also started laughing.

It was maybe around 7:30 am, and the sun at the school was over the hill. You could have seen all of it if it hadn't been covered up by the trees. The light crept through the leaves, and the temperature was nice, although we were both wrapped in a multitude of clothes. Anything under 70 degrees meant my mom was going to be all covered up like a ball of yarn. With layers on layers, colors on colors, and an interesting choice of a comfortable shoe.

Even though my mom's favorite season is summer (she loves the beach and the water, the warmth and all the fun things that come

with summer), I think she reminds me more of fall.

When things turned brown, and she made pumpkin soup, she would bundle me up and give me those huge hugs that felt like getting wrapped in a blanket.

I've mispronounced many things in my life, but this memory sticks with me because my mom is in it.

She always manages to turn even the smallest, silliest moments into something bright. She brings light to my life like one of the many candles we've given her, except warmer, steadier, and impossible to extinguish.

When I first sat down to write this, I thought about doing a poem. I wanted something pretty and poetic enough to match how pretty she is and how much I love her. But the truth is, poetry leaves too much room for misinterpretation, and I need no confusion here.

So I'll say it clearly:

I love you, Mom.

For every laugh, for every layered hug, for every bit of light you've ever given me, for all the care and love you gave me,

and I can't tell you how much I appreciate you.

And that's not me being Star-castic.

That's me being real.

Teracotta Terrace

Playwriting

[Setting: A small, worn kitchen-dining space in a New York apartment, 1996. There is a table and three chairs. Off to the side, a small sitting area with a television. Near stage left is a door and a coat rack with three coats: a man's trenchcoat is among them.]

[Scene 1]

MELVIN Everstein is sitting at the table, newspaper in hand. The headline on the back reads "Tragedy at Teracotta Terrace". CARLY Everstein is sitting nearby. Their son, MOT, enters from stage right, shoulders heavy. He takes a seat at the table.

CARLY
Morning, Mot. Sleep okay?

MOT
Nope.

CARLY
shrugs
That's too bad.

MELVIN slams his newspaper down and stands. He marches to the sink, pours his coffee out while grumbling, and storms toward stage left. CARLY has lowered her eyes. MELVIN snatches his trench coat from a hook, puts it on, and turns back towards MOT.

MELVIN
You think we don't notice, Mot? You think we're slow,
or too tired to see what's going on?

We know you're not home at night. We know the kind of company you keep.

We talk to you, but you don't hear us. You act like you're living in some storybook, but this isn't a fairytale. It's real. You're making it too hard for us to help you.

We work every second of the day, trying to keep this roof over our heads. But that doesn't mean you get to do whatever you want. If you don't want to listen, that's your choice.

But just know, we don't have money for a funeral. *He pauses for emphasis*

So imagin, you lying in an alley, cold and alone, when you could've been here at the table for dinner.

MELVIN exits stage left through the door. CARLY and MOT sit in silence for a moment.

CARLY
[quietly]
He's right. We don't have enough.

CARLY stands and moves to gather her purse, keys, and coat. She exists stage left through the door.

[End Scene]

[Scene 2]

MOT sits on the couch, pensive. RANCH enters stage left and knocks on the door. MOT moves to open it, and RANCH bursts through, loud and energetic.

RANCH
Mot! What's up, man? Last night was wild!

MOT
Yeah. Wild.

RANCH
You alright? You've been talking about getting even for weeks. Now you finally do, and you look like the world just ended...

RANCH moves to the couch and flops down, stretching out like he lives there.

RANCH
That's your problem: nothing's ever enough for you.

MOT moves to sit by RANCH

MOT
Did you come here for something?

RANCH
Yeah. I came to drag you to school. You need it more than anybody I know.

MOT
smirks
You don't even go yourself.

RANCH
Exactly. And even I know better. You don't listen to nobody. Not your folks, not your friends, nobody. You're on your own little path...Guess that means you gotta deal with things your own way, too.

MOT
Yeah, yeah. Let's just go.

They exit stage left.

[End Scene]

[Scene 3]

CARLY enters alone from stage right. She moves to the stage left door and reaches outside to collect the mail. She moves back to the table and sits, flipping through the envelopes. CARLY stops and holds up an envelope marked EVICTION NOTICE. She stares at it with watery eyes before carefully tucking it on the bottom of the pile and setting the stack on the table.

CARLY stands and puts on her work uniform. She moves to the door and opens it, but stops and takes one last look at the apartment. She sighs and exists.

[End Scene 3]

[Scene 4]

MOT and RANCH enter, laughing.

RANCH
—and that's when I told her, "You're lucky I even answered you."

MOT
You really said that?

RANCH
Sure did. She was acting like she paid bills around here.

MOT
You and your brother drive her up the wall. Don't blame her.

RANCH
She's five and already running around like she owns everything. She's so annoying, man.

MOT
laughs
Yeah, okay, Ranch.

MOT grabs a slice of bread. RANCH turns on the TV and drops onto the couch.

RANCH
Hey, look!

MOT turns to the screen.

NEWSCASTER V.O.
We've received confirmation that seventeen young men were killed last night at Terracotta Terrace. Authorities believe it was gang-related violence.

The victims include: Calvin Pater, Matthew Gribly, a boy known as "Little Man," Marvin Alabaster, Lemilton Peach...

The list continues. RANCH and MOT sit frozen until it ends.

RANCH
You heard that, right? He didn't say Aaron.

MOT doesn't respond. He picks up the mail on the table and finds the eviction notice at the bottom. He sighs deeply.

RANCH
So… what are we gonna do about that?

MOT exits stage right. Returns with an envelope full of cash. He sits, counts out bills silently, fifties stacking up. He places it on the table next to the notice. MOT then writes on a sticky note and slaps it on the fridge, lighting a cigarette after.

MOT
Let's go handle it.

They exit through the stage left door.

[End Scene 4]

[Scene 5]

Evening. The kitchen has Chinese takout containers and paper plates on the counter. MELVIN is sitting on the couch, and CARLY is pacing in the kitchen. She has the sticky note in her hand.

CARLY
Still no sign of him?

CARLY sights and starts dishing up a plate of food. MELVIN shakes his head.

MELVIN
Not yet. *sighs* He's been drifting futher every day... I don't know what else to do.

CARLY
We do what we can. That's all we can do.

The phone rings, and CARLY moves to answer. MELVIN turns on the TV.

NEWSCASTER V.O.
Another tragedy this evening in New York. A violent attack at Newman's Inn appears linked to last night's incident of gang violence.

CARLY lifts her hand to her mouth.

NEWSCASTER V.O.
While Police are still identifying the victims and reaching out to their families, we know that among them are Aaron Keeper, Baily Barter, Patrick Baker, Roman Cooling, Myles Reacher, Declan McDonald, Reed Smith, Gregory Price, and a boy known only as "Ranch"...

MELVIN sighs as the caster is talking and stands. He moves to the table and starts sorting through the mail, stopping when he sees the eviction notice and the cash. He looks to CARLY, who has dropped to her knees.

MELVIN moves to CARLY's side. She looks up at him, and he slowly kneels beside her as he realizes. He wraps his arms around her and rocks her.

MELVIN
[chokingly]
I told that boy... we wouldn't have enough for a funeral.

MELVIN breaks down sobbing alongside his wife.

[End Scene]

Then and Now

Acknowledgment

Since my writing is going into a book, I want to give a special shout-out to the ELA teachers who shaped me into the writer and student I am today.

First, to Ms. Bentley: you shaped my mind from the time I was a little kid through fourth grade. You nurtured my curiosity, built my academic foundation, and helped me believe I could be a scholar. I'm incredibly thankful for the time, effort, and care you poured into my learning. Your early impact made a lasting difference in my life.

Next is my mom, who homeschooled me and my twin brother during quarantine, even though I strongly resisted at times because I thought, "I'm at home, not school." That year turned out to be critical. The books we read, the vocab I practiced, and even the long division I learned to love all prepared me for middle school. Despite the chaos of that year, I learned so much, and I'll always appreciate how much you did for us.

Next, to Ms. Langford, my first ELA teacher at a brand-new school. Everything was different from what I was used to, and it was definitely tough at first. But through every mistake and rough draft, you guided me with feedback and support. You helped me realize that ELA wasn't as impossible as I thought. Thank you for challenging me and helping me build the skills that made me better.

To Ms. Lacen: your class was the one I enjoyed most that year. You created a space where I felt heard and inspired. The work I did in your class sparked something in me: I wanted to keep improving. Thank you for introducing me to Hamilton and for giving me

confidence in my voice. With your encouragement and a supportive classroom environment, I grew so much as a writer.

To Ms. Day: your class was the highlight of eighth grade. It was where I got to be creative and expressive more than anywhere else. I wrote pieces that, at the time, were the best I'd ever written. Your lessons were thoughtful, your questions made me think, and you always made me feel seen as a writer. Even when the classroom got chaotic, I knew you hadn't forgotten about me. You helped me believe in my writing and in myself. That confidence didn't stay in your classroom– it followed me everywhere.

Finally, to Mr. Bennett, my ninth and tenth grade ELA teacher: thank you for making writing feel simple and doable. Before your class, essays felt a bit daunting. But the structure you taught us helped everything click. I learned so many small but important things that improved my writing overall. Your class gave me a deeper understanding of literature and taught me how to write more clearly.

ELA has always been something I've loved–reading, writing, criticizing–and thanks to all of you, I've been able to grow in all of those areas. More importantly, the confidence I built in your classrooms has spread into all my other classes. Confidence is key, and because of your teaching, I feel like I can succeed anywhere.

So, thank you: for my skills, for my confidence, and for seeing potential in me before I saw it in myself. One day, when I'm incredibly successful, it'll be because of everything you helped me build.

(Shout out Doc M. "Stay dangerous.")

Adyen Davis

Adyen Davis was born in Georgia and is passionate about wrestling and video games. He dreams of attending Ohio State University and becoming a professional wrestler. Adyen believes in the power of learning and motivation, guided by the motto: "Knowledge is power, and power is money."

The Trouble Kid

Story Excerpt

My name is Malik Darden. I'm from Compton, California–where it's easy to get lost before you even find yourself. Most people around here don't expect much from a kid like me. They see the hoodie, the street I live on, the people I hang around with, and they make up their minds fast.

They call me a 'trouble kid'. I've heard teachers whisper it in the halls, and I see the way security eyes me like I'm always one step away from doing something wrong. But they don't know the whole story.

I'm a multi-sport athlete. I ball hard, basketball and football. And I don't just play–I dominate. I've got offers from real schools: USC, Oregon, UCLA, Texas, Florida State. And just last week, Duke came calling.

Yeah. *Duke.*

Coach Simmons flew all the way out to meet me in person. He sat across from me and my mom in our tiny living room. I could see he was impressed with my film, my stats, my drive. But I could also see something else in his eyes–concern. He didn't waste any time sugarcoating it either.

A Wife's Suspicion

Playwriting

[Scene 1: BRITTANI and DONALD's home.]

BRITTANI is sitting, looking pensive. DONALD is tense. They appear to be mid-discussion. BRITTANI is looking down.

BRITTANI
[quietly]
I hate you and love you at the same time. Isn't that strange?

DONALD
sighs
I know, Brittani.

BRITTANI
You *don't* know. You're hiding something from me. I can feel it.

DONALD
It's not like that...

BRITTANI
[sternly]
Then tell me. Why won't you tell me what's really going on? Are you sick? Dying??

DONALD pauses, conflicted.

DONALD
No, I'm not dying.

BRITTANI
Then what is it? You think I haven't noticed how distand you've been? You sneak out, stay late. You flinch when I ask questions.

DONALD turns away from her.

DONALD
It isn't what you think.

BRITTANI
[tearing up]
I think you're cheating, Donald. And you won't even tell me the truth because you already know that I know.

DONALD pauses.

DONALD
[softly]
I didn't wan to hurt you.

BRITTANI
[angrily]
You *are* hurting me. Every night you don't tell me the truth. That's the *real* pain.

Both stand in silence, the tension thick.

[End Scene]

[Scene 2: A hospital room, three months later]

BRITTANI sits beside DONALD, who lies weak in the hospital bed. The room is dim, quiet, with soft beeping from medical monitors.

BRITTANI
[teary]
You should've told me. We could've faced it together.

DONALD

I didn't want our last days to be full of sadness. I wanted to feel… alive again. And I made some selfish choices.

BRITTANI shakes her head

BRITTANI
You still should've told me the truth.

DONALD
[weakly]
You'll find… a letter… for you. At home. In the drawer by the bed.

Donald closes his eyes. A long pause. The heart monitor flatlines.

[End Scene]

[Scene 3: BRITTANI and DONALD's bedroom]

BRITTANI is sitting on the bed. She opens a drawer and pulls out a sealed envelope with her name on it.

BRITTANI (reading)
"My love,

If you're reading this, I'm already gone. I know you're angry, and you have every right to be. I did cheat–but not for love or lust. I had cancer, and I made a bucket list. It was stupid, reckless, and I know it hurt you. I was scared, Brittani. Not of dying–but of you watching me fade away.

But the truth is, every moment with you was the best part of my life. I never stopped loving you. Not even for a second.

I left you $350,000 with my insurance. It won't fix what I broke, but maybe it can help you build something new. Something beautiful–just like you.

Forgive me if you can.

Love, always, Donald."

[End Scene.]

Madison Dismukes

Madison Dismukes is from Chicago, and she brings her creativity and competitive spirit to everything she does. She enjoys playing sports and designing nails and plans to attend Southern University with goals of achieving success and wealth. Madison loves writing drama and horror stories and lives by the mantra: "Keep writing, keep living, keep loving."

Sophmore Year

Poem

Sophomore year, where do I even start?
Kinda tough, but played a huge part.
Lots of new classes, tryna find my way,
Hoping that I make it through each day.
Friends by my side, we're learning a lot
Late-night talks and crazy memories.
Learned some stuff, laughed a lot too,
Sophomore year, I kinda enjoyed you.
Almost there, halfway done,
High school's like a marathon.
Gonna keep pushing, gotta stay true,
Sophomore year, thank you for being you.

Flag Football

Short Story

This past February was my second year of flag football. Our flag football team was getting even more serious. We were all about making it to state, since this year was Tennessee's first girls' flag football state championship! Practices were brutal; it was a lot of ups and downs, but it was all worth it! We were so happy because we made it to state! We were one of the first 16 girls' teams in Tennessee to go to state.

The season was definitely a rollercoaster. Some games we did excellently, others were super close and stressful, and we lost. But every win got us closer to state, and every loss made us tougher, and we knew what to do better next time. By May, we were doing great, making it through regionals and the championship. We were so happy to be one of the first teams to play for the first-ever girls flag football state title.

State was very competitive! The competition was way different, and even though we didn't win, it was still the best experience ever. I had so much fun meeting new people and learning new things! We made history just by being there. All the hard work, the dedication, the fun, and even the stress was worth it. It was a season I'll never forget. Junior year next!

Justyn Harris

Justyn Harris was born in Tennessee and is preparing to attend High School. He aspires to major in entrepreneurship and pursue a career as either a professional NFL or NBA player. Justyn is passionate about sports and building a successful future.

Bloom

Poetry

Life can bruise with storm and friction, Winds that shake the roots of life. Darkness remains, shadows stay– Hope feels lost and swept away.

But in the cracks where sorrows pace, New light breaks through pain's thread trace. A bloom can rise from ruined ground, Where silence once was the only sound.

The hurt that carves can shape us too, Into something strong and true. For even night must end in day, And joy can grow in sorrow's clay.

Some things might be sad and cruel, But throughout life, your time will bloom.

The Untold

Short Story

She was the kind of girl you could pass on the street and never notice— but that was the point. After everything she had been through, blending into the crowd was survival. The past wasn't just a memory for Ava, it was a haunting. The type of thing that never stayed buried, no matter how deep you shoveled.

Ava moved to the city to start over. New name. New job. New apartment with locks she double-checked every night. Her days were quiet, measured, forgettable—until she met him.

Liam.

He had a quiet charm, the kind that sneaks up on you. He wasn't flashy or loud; he listened. Really listened. Ava didn't even remember telling him about her favorite poetry book or how she hated the smell of lavender, but somehow, he remembered. He noticed things no one else did.

That should've been sweet.

But with every kind gesture, every perfectly timed message, Ava felt both attached to him and disturbed. Disturbed by the feeling that he was always a step ahead. Like he knew her before she knew herself.

He made her feel seen, and that terrified her.

Because Ava wasn't sure she wanted to be seen. Not fully. Not with the kind of past she carried.

There were gaps in her memory, yes, but not in her pain: The foster homes. The manipulative stepfather. The nights she flinched when someone knocked on her door.

She was twelve. Hiding in the back of the linen closet, her knees drawn up to her chest. The door cracked open just enough to let in the hallway light. Footsteps thudded closer. Her stepfather's voice—low, impatient—echoed down the corridor.

"Ava. Come out. Now."

She held her breath. She didn't cry. She had learned silence was safer than pleading.

The footsteps stopped right outside the door.

A creak.

A pause.

Then, retreating steps. The moment they faded, she stayed still, counting to two hundred before she dared move.

She never told anyone. Just like all the other times.

Liam was the first person who made her feel safe. That scared her more than anything.

She tried to pull away. She told herself she wasn't ready. That she didn't deserve someone like him.

But Liam didn't take distance well.

He said he understood, but his eyes told a different story. When she didn't text back, he showed up at her favorite coffee shop. When she unfollowed him, he made a new account. When she asked for space, he gave her poetry that mirrored her exact thoughts.

How did he know?

The truth was, Liam had been watching Ava long before she ever knew his name.

It started six months before they'd even met.

Liam was sitting in his usual corner at the bookstore, a tiny independent shop nestled between an antique store and a café, when he first saw her. She was standing in the horror section, her hands trembling slightly as she flipped through the pages of a book she would never remember reading. Her hair clung to her face, rainwater streaming down her jacket, pooling at her feet like a reflection of the sadness in her eyes.

He had noticed her immediately. Not because of her beauty—though she was beautiful, in a quiet way—but because of the way she held herself. Like she was trying to disappear. Like she couldn't stand to be seen yet couldn't stop herself from reaching out to something that might offer escape.

Liam didn't believe in fate. But he believed in people who needed saving.

And Ava? She looked like a soul begging to be rescued.

He'd watched her from across the room, studying her, piecing together the fragments of her life he could observe from afar. How she avoided eye contact with the staff, how she picked up books but never took them to the counter, how she seemed to recoil when anyone came too close. But it wasn't just her behavior. It was the way she carried herself: like the weight of the world was on her shoulders, but she didn't know how to ask for help.

Liam had always been the type to notice people like that. People who were falling apart but didn't know how to let anyone in. It was his curse, really. He couldn't walk away from someone who needed him.

So he followed her out into the rain, watched her disappear

down the street, her silhouette blurred by the droplets. He didn't approach her then—he couldn't. But he'd taken mental notes of her patterns, her habits.

The next day, he followed her again, just to see if she'd return to the same bookstore. She did. And again, the next week. And the week after that. Slowly, he built a profile of her: where she went, what she liked, what triggered her smiles, what kept her on edge.

He learned that she liked poetry, though she kept it hidden. He saw her at a local café one evening, tucked into a corner booth, her nose buried in a collection of Rumi's poems. And at that moment, Liam knew exactly how to reach her. He started leaving small, cryptic notes in places she couldn't ignore: a page torn from a book she had once been reading; a napkin from the café with a single line of poetry written on it.

He wasn't stalking her, he told himself. He was saving her.

Ava never stood a chance.

The first time they actually spoke was at a bookstore of all places. Liam had seen her perusing the same horror section, looking lost in her thoughts. He approached her, offering a book she hadn't seen before, knowing the exact title that would catch her attention. The way her eyes lit up when she read the title, how she hesitated just long enough before accepting the book, made him smile inside.

She was just as he expected. A little broken. A little hesitant. But still so damn beautiful.

It wasn't until the following week that things took a darker turn. Ava didn't show up at the bookstore. Nor did she show up the week after that.

Liam couldn't have that. He needed her.

So he showed up at the coffee shop where she often sat, pretending it was by chance. She looked at him with wide eyes, startled by his presence, but there was something else there—

something that told him she wasn't just surprised. She was relieved.

He didn't know why. But he knew that feeling. The need to be found. To be saved.

And Ava needed saving.

But as Ava began to heal–to reclaim pieces of herself–the carefully constructed facade of Liam began to crack. She started asking questions. Digging. And the more she learned, the more she realized:

She wasn't in love. She was in danger.

She had seen the texts. The ones from his "old friend" that always seemed to be written with perfect timing. The ones that mirrored her exact emotions, her exact fears. She had asked him once, nervously, how he always knew what she needed before she said a word. He had smiled, telling her that he paid attention to the little things.

But there were too many little things. Too many things he shouldn't have known.

The poetry, the strange coincidences, the way he seemed to know exactly where she'd be before she did– it wasn't normal. It was suffocating.

She started pushing back, little by little. She unfollowed him on social media, then changed her privacy settings. But Liam didn't take the hint. He made new accounts. He showed up uninvited, knocking on her door at strange hours. He texted her when she hadn't responded in days, sending long, rambling messages about fate and destiny.

Liam had been watching Ava long before she ever knew his name. And to him, she was still that lost girl in the rain. Still in need of his protection. Still his to fix–even if it meant breaking her first.

Ava realized then that she wasn't just afraid of him. She was terrified

of herself. Terrified of how deeply he had rooted himself inside her life.

And when Liam finally cornered her in her own apartment, his words barely audible over the pounding of her heart, Ava knew there was only one way out.

She had to disappear again.

The Blood Key

Playwriting

Characters–
LENA: A strong-willed, brave 16-year-old girl
RAFAEL: Her estranged father, a feared drug lord
CAPTAIN VEGA: A police officer hunting Rafael
GUARD: One of Rafael's men

[Scene 1: A dark, locked basement]

LENA is tied to a chair; dirty, bruised, and cut, she listens carefully. GUARD enters to bring food. As he turns his back, she kicks him hard, causing him to drop the keys. She scrambles for them despite being barely able to move.)

GUARD
Hey, stop!

LENA stabs him with a sharp metal piece from the chair; he falls. She grabs the keys, unlocks the door, and flees.

[End Scene]

[Scene 2: A manor hall]

LENA sneaks through the corridor. She hears voices and hides behind a column. Looking for somewhere to hide, she slips into a room and sees a man behind a desk: RAFAEL.

RAFAEL
You've grown up. I wondered when you'd find your way here.

LENA
[furious]
You had me taken. Why?!

RAFAEL
To keep you close. You're my daughter: you were born to lead this empire.

LENA
I'd rather burn with it than take over.

LENA pulls a hidden gun from her waistband. RAFAEL calmly raises a hand.

RAFAEL
You think I fear death? I've lived in it. But I am your father; you carry my blood.

LENA
Then I'll spill it.

[End Scene]

[Scene 3: A warehouse outside the mansion]

CAPTAIN VEGA waits with a squad. LENA appears with blood on her shirt.

LENA
He's inside. You have one shot. He won't run, he wants a legacy.

CAPTAIN VEGA
You sure you want him alive?

LENA
He dies, but not yet. I need the world to see what monsters call themselves fathers.

LENA hands over a flash drive.

LENA
This has everything. Name's "Routes Money"

CAPTAIN VEGA
You're a brave kid.

LENA
I'm not a kid anymore.

[End Scene]

[Scene 4: Outside the manor]

RAFAEL is arrested in handcuffs. LENA watches silently.

RAFAEL
You are your mother's revenge.

LENA
No. I'm mine.

LENA turns and walks into the dawn with the officers.

[End Scene]

Anijah Hatten

Anijah Hatten is a recent high school graduate, where she was a part of the Design and Tech Academy. Passionate about creativity and self-growth, she enjoys nature adventures and listening to music in her free time. Anijah is enthusiastic about building her communication and writing skills, gaining valuable work experience, and taking on new responsibilities. She looks forward to connecting with others and using this opportunity as a stepping stone toward a successful college journey.

What About Now?

Poetry

Here, There, Everywhere…
Sometimes I tend to really never care,

Dazing off into the possible beauty of tomorrow
The days, weeks, and months all start blend into one

So much to the point I feel like I'm living in a fairytale…
Almost making life into a haze

Appreciating the breeze and beginning to go with the flow of the now
I guide myself down my path of dreams and see what it has to offer me

Dream, Dream, Dream,
Can you please be a bit of serene

Please, rip me from the chaos of what could've been or what can be
And just place me into the now, Ms. Serene

Why Feeling Lost Might Mean You're on the Right Path

Article Writing, Informal

What am I (doing)?

I feel like when you're lost in life is when you're the most found...

Why do I say that, you ask?

Because the art of life is the never-ending cycle of learning.

If you feel like you're found, maybe you haven't experienced enough to really know what living life is like!

It's all about those roller coaster moments that teach you what to do and what not to do when moving forward in life.

All of those moments in your life are the most vital steps to push you to see what's on the other side of the unknowing.

In moments when you feel lost and confused in life, take a minute to focus on the bigger picture.

Step outside of yourself and analyze what you're doing if you think you're making a mistake, and give thanks for that perspective.

Once you have awareness and can pinpoint the mistake, accept it as is.

Understand that there is a greater reason as to why you aren't getting something right in that moment and go with the flow.

Be okay with making that mistake.

Once you fully accept what it is– rather than what you think it should be –youll discover that this acceptance is what it means to truly be.

Don't dig too deep... just deep enough to analyze what you think is wrong and put forth the action to learn the lesson that is being taught by the experience.

It is necessary to be "lost" and "wrong" to be guided to the path of the right and righteousness.

Your wrongs and confusion are the guides that teach you what you need to change moving forward. Be okay with not knowing everything and not sticking to what's comfortable and familiar to you. Trust that the strange and unknown things will guide you to your truest self.

Once you break the cycle of your knowing, and step into the unknown, endless possibilities and opportunities will arise to help you create and live the life you really want!

Next time you feel lost, try embracing it– your next chapter may just be starting!

Kadiyah Inmon

Kadiyah was born in Michigan and currently attends high school. She enjoys doing hair, playing volleyball, and writing about young adult life. With dreams of becoming a doctor, Kadiyah is passionate about helping others while expressing herself creatively. Her outlook on life is captured in her favorite quote: "To truly live is to embrace the moments, forget the past's weight, and live unreservedly—for in love, we find the essence of our existence.

Who Am I

Poetry

I wake up every morning, feeling so confused,
Like I don't know myself, like I've been used.
One day I want to be one thing, the next I change my mind,
Trying to find who I am, but I'm so hard to find.
My friends say I'm cool, but inside I feel lost,
Like I'm paying a price for what I thought I'd never cost.
Sometimes I hide my feelings, afraid to be real,
Wondering if someday I'll know how I feel.
I wish I could just understand who I'm supposed to be,
But right now, I'm just a kid, searching for me.
Maybe someday I'll find out, I'll be okay,
Until then, I'll keep trying, day after day.

The Talent Show

Short Story

In the bustling streets of Seoul, 2010, JK often wandered through the crowded markets and lively neighborhoods, feeling a quiet sense of doubt about himself. Despite the vibrant energy around him, he carried a shadow of insecurity, convinced he lacked any special talents. His friends Tae and Mike, noticing his quiet reluctance, decided to sign him up for the school's talent show.

One afternoon, as they gathered near the school, Tae and Mike casually mentioned the upcoming talent show, hinting that it would be fun if JK participated. JK hesitated, unsure of what he could possibly do on stage.

"I-I don't know, guys," JK announced.

Tae quickly replied, "Aw, c'mon, JK, you sing and dance really well!"

"Yeah, and we will be there supporting you," Mike added.

"O-ok I guess," JK unsurely said while scratching his head. His friends' insistence made him agree—though deep down, he still doubted himself. He was very anxious, since he only had five days to perfect his performance.

The day of the show arrived with the gymnasium packed with students. This started to panic JK; he began sweating heavily. Confused on what to do, JK ran to the school basement, hoping he would calm down there.

Meanwhile, Tae and Mike were patiently waiting for JK to perform, completely oblivious to everything. The host, Mr. Jay, had finally

called JK's name as he was the last one to perform. Not a single soul moved to the center of the stage. Students began questioning each other about what was happening, but no single person had an answer. Tae went looking for JK, while Mike was calling and texting him. JK was nowhere to be found.

Tae and Mike had to move swiftly in order to find JK and still have time for him to go on stage. They knew that he couldn't leave the school building, so that was a big relief for them. Searching every single bathroom, JK was nowhere to be found.

JK

I had run to the school basement hoping to calm down from my anxiety. Hearing the crowd cheer had me super nervous. The basement was always my safe spot, especially when I was overwhelmed. I forgot the door locks from the outside when shut all the way. I quickly ran to the door and began banging on it and yelling.

"Help me! I'm stuck in here!"

After five minutes of calling for help, I felt useless and like I was never going to get out. I decided to try one last time; giving my all, I kicked the door really hard, creating a loud bang.

Fortunately, Tae was passing by the basement door when JK kicked it. Tae was startled but decided to investigate the noise. He went to the door and began pulling it back, which created a loud scratching sound. JK heard the noise of the door and quickly ran to it.

"H-hello, who is there?" Tae asked.

"Oh my gosh Tae, thank you for saving me, I was stuck down here!" JK excitedly said while hugging Tae.

“Why were you down here? They are calling your name to perform right now,” Tae said.

“I accidentally locked myself down here trying to calm down for the talent show,” JK explained.

Tae looked at JK with a mixture of concern and reassurance. “You okay now? We need to get you upstairs before it’s too late.”

JK nodded quickly, trying to catch his breath and steady his nerves. “Yeah, I’m fine now. Sorry for causing so much trouble.”

Mike suddenly appeared at the top of the stairs, catching his breath from running around. “There you are, JK! We’ve been looking everywhere. Mr. Jay is waiting for you!”

JK hesitated, a wave of fear washing over him again. “I... I don’t think I can do it anymore,” he whispered, eyes wide with anxiety.

Tae gently placed a hand on JK’s shoulder. “Hey, you don’t have to be perfect. Just be yourself. That’s enough.”

Mike nodded supportively. “We believe in you, JK. Just take a deep breath and go out there. No matter what happens, we’re proud of you for even trying.”

Gathering his courage, JK took a deep breath, feeling the warmth of his friends’ support. He nodded slowly, ready to step back onto the stage.

As they led him out of the basement and toward the gymnasium, JK felt a flicker of confidence ignite inside him. Maybe he wasn’t as talentless as he thought. Maybe, just maybe, he had a little bit of courage after all.

When JK finally stepped onto the stage, the bright lights made his heart race, but he remembered Tae and Mike’s words. With a tentative smile, he began to sing softly, his voice growing steadier with each note. The crowd listened, captivated by the courage shining through his performance. By the end of his song, the

applause was loud and warm. JK looked out at the smiling faces and realized that sometimes, the greatest talent is simply having the bravery to face your fears.

And from that day on, JK knew that even in the busiest streets of Seoul, he could find strength within himself, especially when surrounded by friends who believed in him.

Jaliyah Jarrett

Jaliyah Jarrett is a Nashville native and a standout student. She is passionate about law and hopes to attend Belmont University to become a patent lawyer. Inspired by Ralph Waldo Emerson's quote, "The only person you are destined to become is the person you decide to be," Jaliyah is focused on shaping her own future.

She has built strong problem-solving and critical thinking skills through playing basketball, writing poetry, and taking photographs. Her favorite scripture, "I can do all things through Christ who strengthens me" (Philippians 4:13), keeps her motivated and grounded as she works hard toward her goals.

Off the Right Track?

Poetry

The world continued, a colorful, unwavering dynamic orb
While Kiara stood apart, suspended, broken, lost in her core
Utterly consumed by fear
With seemingly no end near
Not the usual fear of animals, of dark or death
But the quiet fear of vanishing out of sight

It started small, a voice on a chilly breeze
"What's next for you?" During a cold day in fall
Every friend had an option, so obvious, so clear
But the question echoed deeper in her ear
It felt like survival masked as freedom–
Like every step could tip the balance

Being an African American woman
Was like walking through fog
With mirrors on all sides
Leaving the reflection distorted–
Truth bent by someone else's light
A light too harsh to discover her own path.

She walked; was she choosing or just staying alive?

A hazy landscape where dreams and peril blurred
Even memory betrayed her
Was she ever on trajectory?
Or had she been walking in circles

Chasing shadows of what she could have been?

She stopped–
Not from weariness
But because something shifted

A sound, not wind.
Not voice.
But known.

A scraping, low and steady
Nearer…

She slowly turned,
And there through fog
A shadow loomed

Not hers.

Not alone.

And it spoke her name
But not the same
Not like they did.

The Unseen Hand: How Media Shapes Our Ideas about Race and Supports Racism

Article Writing, Outline

James Baldwin once said, "You don't hate people unless you fear them. And you can't fear them unless you think you know them." But what if everything you think you know is based on lies?

Racism is not kept alive only by hate; it persists in subtle, devious media bias. Through television news and entertainment shows, the media creates what we believe about other people. Not only does it represent the world, it builds the world. Too often, the media continues to perpetuate negative stereotypes and subtle prejudice.

One of the earliest examples was the minstrel show. White performers acting in blackface stereotyped Black people in the 1800s and established such characters as 'Jim Crow' and 'Mammy'. These racist caricatures popularized slavery and dehumanization. Although the format fell out of favor, the stereotypes reappeared in films, radio, and television. Native Americans were made into 'savages', Asian Americans 'exotic' or 'model minorities'. These portraits solidified into cultural run-downs that still affect how we think.

How Media Sustains Racism

The insidious ability of media to influence racial opinion can be broken down into some basic processes:

- Stereotypes and Space: Minoritized groups are rendered invisible or reduced to stereotypes, like the 'angry Black man' or 'nerdy Asian', limiting public information.
- Framing: Crime news usually equates violence with color. Biased language such as "thug" and biased reporting frames opinion.
- Stories: With dominant white writers, stories will erase or distort minoritized peoples' histories.
- Implicit Bias: Reusing images socializes our unconscious bias, which affects hiring, justice, and daily life.

Why It Matters: The Harmful Consequences

The impact of media bias goes far beyond mere misrepresentation: it causes serious and long-term harm to individuals and society. It does this by:

- Legitimizing prejudice and sustaining deeply ingrained biases.
- Distorting perception and misleading the inexperienced.
- Destroying self-esteem of oppressed people.
- Producing division by creating fear and inequality.

What Needs to Change

For the deep impact of the media in reinscribing racism to change, there must be a radical and widespread shift of practice and thinking by industry and public. Potential solutions include:

- Diverse Storytellers: Several creators need to be hired for authentic stories.
- Critical Thinking: Individuals should critically question messages in the media.
- More Representation: The media must represent richer, fuller lives, not stereotypes.
- Amplify Voices: Permit marginalized groups to speak for

themselves.

Conclusion

Media has been propelling racism forward behind closed doors, insidiously shaping our perception and cementing toxic stereotypes. But this vast influence can also be used to fight against the harm. If it was employed to construct injustice, it can most certainly be utilized to unravel it by being committed to sharing authentic, diverse, and empowering narratives. A fairer, wealthier world begins with better narratives.

Je'Corean Lee

Je'Corean Lee is from Nashville, Tennessee, and has a strong passion for athletics. He participates in football, basketball, track, and working out. Hoping to attend Ohio State, Je'Corean dreams of playing professional football. While he prefers drawing over writing, he values hard work and believes: "If you do the bare minimum, you'll receive the bare minimum."

My Family's Forgotten Treasure

Short Story

My family has always been a mystery. We weren't really *rich*, as you might say, yet my grandfather always managed to be *seen* as rich. My grandfather and I have been close since I was young, doing all sorts of things together. Our adventures were filled with laughter and learning, whether we were exploring the woods behind his house or simply sitting by the fireplace as he recounted tales from his youth.

His stories were always imbued with wisdom, subtly guiding me to become the person I am today. He taught me the importance of perseverance, integrity, and curiosity. Unfortunately, his time came. Before he passed, he told me about our family's "Forgotten Treasure." In his honor, I set out on a journey to find the treasure, facing many challenges including food, shelter, warmth, and more, but eventually overcoming them with self-reliance and strength until I found a trail.

The choice of location for the treasure was deeply symbolic: a place where my grandfather and I had spent hours together, sharing stories, dreams, and laughter. By hiding the treasure here, he ensured that finding it would not only be a physical discovery, but also a journey back to the strength of our relationship.

Venturing inside, I was faced with traps like flying arrows, pitfalls, swinging blades, and poisonous gases. Overcoming these challenges, I soon discovered the treasure: a plain watch, with no diamonds, that my grandfather used to wear. Yet it bore the memory of wisdom; while others may find it worthless, I knew it truly was my family's "forgotten treasure."

The Echoes of Harmony

Playwriting

Characters–

EMILY: A passionate young musician determined to bring back the music festival.
MR. THOMPSON: The suspicious caretaker who's seen it all.
SARAH: Emily's encouraging friend, always by her side.
MAYOR JOHNSON: The practical mayor, focused on the budget.
MRS. GREEN: A retired music teacher with a wealth of experience.

ACT 1: ENCOURAGEMENT

[Scene 1: Community Hall Stage]

EMILY stands on the stage, looking over the dusty instruments.

EMILY
It's been ages since we had the festival. We need to bring music back!

MR. THOMPSON walks in.

MR. THOMPSON
Dreaming big again, Emily?

EMILY
We can totally revive it! Just think of the joy it'll bring.

MR. THOMPSON
Times have changed. I'm not sure people care anymore.

[End Scene]

[Scene 2: Mayor's Office]

EMILY and SARAH are sitting down with MAYOR JOHNSON.

EMILY
Let's bring the festival back! It'll lift everyone's spirits!

MAYOR JOHNSON
The budget is pretty tight. We just can't swing it right now.

SARAH
What if we look for sponsors?

MAYOR JOHNSON
If you can secure some funding, I'll back you up.

[End Scene]

ACT 2: HARMONY

[Scene 1: MRS. GREEN's house.]

EMILY
How did you pull off the festival in the past?

MRS. GREEN
It was all about the community coming together.

EMILY
Would you help us organize it again?

MRS. GREEN
I'd love to! Let's rally some volunteers.

[End Scene.]

[Scene 2: Town Square]

EMILY and SARAH gather townspeople.

EMILY
We need your support to bring the festival back!
Who's in?

Townspeople start to step forward to volunteer.

[End Scene]

[Scene 3: Community Hall Stage, Festival Day]

The town buzzes with music. EMILY stands ready to take the stage.

EMILY
Thank you all for believing in this dream. Let's make it a day to remember!

The festival kicks off, uniting the town in a beautiful harmony.

Understanding COVID-19: Key Points

Article Writing

COVID-19, caused by the SARS-CoV-2 virus, has had a major global impact. Here are three essential points to consider:

Transmission and Prevention: The virus spreads mainly through respiratory droplets from coughs, sneezes, or talking. Preventative measures include wearing masks, social distancing, hand hygiene like alcohol, and good ventilation. Vaccination plays an important role in reducing disease severity and preventing others from visiting the hospital.

Symptoms and Health Impact: Symptoms range from mild fever, cough, and fatigue to severe pneumonia and/or organ failure. Vulnerable groups, such as older adults and those with already diagnosed conditions, face higher risks. Long-term effects, known as "long COVID," can affect individuals even after recovery.

Societal and Economic Effects: The pandemic strained healthcare systems and disrupted economies, leading to job losses and increased reliance on digital communication such as phones, computers, and remote work. Education shifted online, highlighting the loss in community access.

Understanding these aspects is significant for managing COVID-19 and preparing for future health challenges. Preventative measures and vaccination efforts remain key to controlling the pandemic.

Londyn McDonald

Londyn is an aspiring poet from Pontiac, Michigan. She draws inspiration from reading deeply meaningful books, especially poetry, and finds that writing helps her feel better and more connected to herself. She was drawn to this program because it offered a refreshing and meaningful way to spend her summer.

What Lies Ahead

Poetry

As of right now
I know where I'm headed.
I know where my future
is taking me.

I anticipate the future
that I'm carving for myself.
Although some things are missing,
I know it's set in stone.

My patient waiting
has become a virtue,
yet it still gets away
from me at times.

My uncertainty blooms
like a summer flower in June,
and my hands
begin to shake once more.

Suddenly, my soul
feels lost again,
like it was
when I was younger.

Suddenly, there's a voice
whispering in my ear

that the loudest music
can't drown out.

It tells me
I should be scared.
Scared of what
the future may bring.

Fortunately, though,
anticipation is stronger.
It fills me
with excitement.

Because my life
is seemingly
only getting better,
with little left uncertain.

Sure, there are some things
that I'm unsure of,
that's just a given
in the future.

You will never know everything,
and that's alright.
but you should anticipate
the things you do

The Girl in the Mirror

Poetry

You wonder why you can never rest
when a frown always greets your mirror.
You see your reflection, and you think
"I don't like anything about her."

"I don't like her hooded eyes,
or the blemish on her cheek.
I don't like the discoloration
painted on her front teeth."

You scrutinize every detail,
the things others wouldn't notice.
You say you need to fix them
but what you really need to know is

no one cares like you think.
Just watch and you'll see.
You'll see people just like you
who aren't afraid to be.

Be the person that they are,
so uniquely their own.
The person they were made to be,
from the soul to the bone.

When you see someone true to themself
you can't help your envy.

You can't help thinking to yourself
"If I would only let me."

If you would only let you,
let your true self emerge,
you'd finally be satisfied
instead of living on the verge.

The verge of self-destruction
as you shut yourself away.
becoming someone that you aren't,
anxiety begging you to stay.

Stay in the "comfort" of discomfort,
the constant hating yourself.
Self-scrutiny becoming routine
wishing you were someone else.

This cycle can be tough to break,
trust me, I would know.
but if you take the time you need
you will reap what you sow.

Start by looking in the mirror
and greeting it with a smile.
If you do that everyday day
it will start to run a mile.

The scrutiny will eventually cease
and you will rise anew.
Rise up from where you shut yourself,
and find the new you.

But hopefully it's not completely new.
Hopefully, some things stay the same.
From your soul to your bone,

the same girl that shares your name.

Giliam Primero Mejia

Giliam Primero Mejia hopes to continue his education at Belmont University and pursue a career in structural engineering. While writing isn't his favorite activity, Giliam expresses his individuality with confidence. His personal motto: "We are not horses, we are humans—we are."

A Taste of Heaven

Poetry

Each bite sends you into a state of shock and pleasure
Making you crave more
the culinary action that motivates
your mouth for another bite

The Compromise

Short Story

Once upon a time, in a prehistoric world where dinosaurs thrived, the dynamic fabric of existence was on the verge of a monumental shift. A remarkable and elegant alien spacecraft emerged from the depths of a swirling, cloudy sky, signifying its descent into a vibrant world filled with breathtaking ancient creatures. The alien itself was a sight to behold, showcasing glimmering skin that sparkled under the warm embrace of the sun, with curious features that set it apart from anything on Earth. Bright, vivid colors adorned its form, painting a vision of extraordinary lands and experiences waiting to be discovered. The astonishing figure soon formed an unexpected yet heartwarming bond with the dinosaurs, displaying a connection that transcended the boundaries of nature. Much to the astonishment of the alien's friends, the dinosaurs and the alien engaged in delightful adventures, with sounds of laughter rising through the air like music. The other aliens soon joined. They frolicked across expansive landscapes bursting with vibrant plant life and breathtaking vistas, creating heartfelt connections as they thrived together in joyful exploration. The larger dinosaurs, embodying a spirit of camaraderie and adventure, generously allowed the aliens to ride on their massive backs, painting a beautiful picture of unity amid diversity.

Unfortunately, this idyllic existence would not last. It came to a shattering halt when a confrontation erupted between one of the aliens and a particularly aggressive dinosaur, known for its fierce dominance over its territory. This clash ignited a tragic series of events that led to the pioneering alien's untimely demise—a loss that deeply impacted both communities and sent shockwaves

reverberating through their intertwined destinies. In a passionate response to the loss of their cherished friend, the remaining dinosaurs, driven by rage and sorrow, mobilized against the aliens, leading to a war that lasted an agonizing fifty years. This was a painful chapter, forever etched in their memories, highlighting a conflict once rooted in friendship, now spiraled into grief.

As the relentless fighting dragged on, various factions arose amid the turmoil, each group from the dinosaurs and aliens genuinely yearning for peace and seeking to bring an end to the devastation that had shattered their lives. Yet, their path toward unity was fraught with difficulties, as the growing tensions and divergent interests complicated their attempts to find common ground. The war extended far beyond anyone's imagination, leaving the once-inquisitive dinosaurs to ponder their existence during a rare month-long ceasefire. This temporary reprieve provided an opportunity for reflection and dialogue. During this period, generals from both factions gathered under the soft glow of flickering candlelight, sharing their stories and engaging in earnest discussions to uncover the causes of their violent rift. They sought answers about the alien's supposed aggression and aimed to unravel the misunderstandings that brought about their shared suffering. With a determined spirit to discover the truth and learn from their past missteps, they resolved to investigate further while maintaining the ceasefire, united by a mutual desire to restore harmony.

The investigation proved to be a challenging undertaking, demanding unwavering commitment and collaboration from both sides. Despite numerous hurdles, after extensive dialogue and efforts, they stumbled upon a stunning revelation: the alien had not acted from malice but was compelled to confront their territory due to the influence of a hidden third party that had instigated their conflicts from the very beginning. Upon grasping this startling realization, leaders from both communities reconvened, carefully considering their subsequent actions. Should they persist in fighting the aliens, who had been unjustly implicated in the strife that wrought so much pain and destruction? In a pivotal moment of

clarity, they collectively resolved to confront this enigmatic third party, known only as "The X"— the true catalyst of the discord that had disrupted their worlds.

With a firm sense of purpose and unity, the coalition of leaders embarked on a significant expedition to discover The X's home planet, aspiring to negotiate reparations and address the extensive damage caused by the chaotic war. However, the earnest pleas for assistance were unexpectedly met with strong resistance, igniting hostilities that had, for a brief moment, settled down. After enduring years of relentless strife, both communities teetered on the brink of exhaustion, as warriors grew weary and hearts ached under the burden of grief. In this critical moment, The X ultimately capitulated, bringing an end to the prolonged agony that had tormented both civilizations.

In the aftermath of the war that had torn them apart, the surviving dinosaurs and aliens set about the challenging task of reconstructing their societies. Unified in their efforts, they dedicated themselves to healing the wounds inflicted during the tragic conflict, diligently working side by side to mend the significant damage wrought by their tumultuous history.

How is Chernobyl After Years of Seclusion?

Article Writing, Formal

Chernobyl, Ukraine, experienced a catastrophic disaster in 1986, ultimately resulting in monumental devastation that claimed numerous lives and left many others injured. The events surrounding this tragic incident continue to promote curiosity and concern, leading many to wonder what Chernobyl looks like today, years after its infamous past, and whether it is now safe to return and visit this historic site that holds such sorrowful memories.

To understand the current state of Chernobyl, one must first revisit how this horrific tragedy began. On April 26, 1986, a catastrophic failure occurred during a routine safety test involving a reactor at the Chernobyl Nuclear Power Plant. This failure ignited a series of events, culminating in a massive steam explosion that threw radioactive materials into the atmosphere. This unexpected release led to widespread contamination and forest devastation, not only profoundly affecting the surrounding region but also extending its influence far beyond through radioactive fallout. The impact was immediate and severe, resulting in mass evacuations and long-term health issues for many—some of these health issues were vomiting, nausea, weakness, fatigue, and fever—which left a legacy that would resonate for generations.

Fast forward to 2025: Chernobyl has transformed into a site that, while still steeped in its tragic history, is considered safe for visitation under certain conditions. Some individuals have even returned to live within the city's borders, seeking to reconnect with

their homeland despite the lingering remnants of the past. However, numerous areas remain abandoned, and while safety protocols have improved, small amounts of radiation are still detectable in parts of the landscape. Former residents who have bravely chosen to come back to their homes might find it comforting to see familiar surroundings yet must consider that children are generally prohibited from residing there due to ongoing safety concerns regarding radiation exposure. This duality of life within Chernobyl—the blend of returning residents and isolated remnants—paints a compelling picture of a place that embodies both the resilience of the human spirit and the need to respect and acknowledge the sorrows of the past.

Ismaeel Moskinzada

Ismaeel Moskinzada is a multi-talented student who enjoys rock climbing, reading, writing fiction, coding, hiking, and photography. A member of both his school's rock climbing and Quizbowl teams, Ismaeel finds joy in solving problems through code and connecting with others through stories. He dreams of one day helping people through his career while making time for family, spirituality, and creativity. He is currently working on finishing his novel and believes that storytelling helps us remember who we are and understand the world around us.

Selected Haikus

Poetry

Religion
I hope to follow
My religion perfectly.
I'll start by praying.

Effort
I want to work hard
Always. It's hard, with my mind.
But I won't give up.

So Much
I feel lost, alone.
Confused on how to manage
Stress and disorders.

Ducks in the Dark

Short Story

It was late. Not later than usual, mind you, but that didn't get rid of the uneasiness. *Breathe. You know you have to do this. It will help,* I attempted to reassure myself—after all, this evening routine was the only time I felt truly calm, truly safe. The sky was pitch black, the trees and foliage of the park being little more than grey-colored silhouettes. I walked along the path until I reached the pond. I sat near the water, cross-legged. It, too, was black, save the reflection from the streetlights. I took off my backpack and reached into it, bringing out a bag filled with peas. Slowly, pulled out the pieces and threw them into the water. I watched the pond, hoping that they would come to me. Slowly, one by one, ducks came into the light. I saw them—shimmering green, stunningly brown, and beautifully white. As they began to eat the peas, I felt the sense of calm I had been seeking. Suddenly, a bright light flashed before my eyes. My heart stopped, then began to beat rapidly, the feeling rising up my chest and into my throat. I heard a voice, loud and angry.

"What are you doing here? If you don't get off this property, I swear to God I'll put a bullet between your eyes!"

I couldn't see who was in front of me, and I struggled to breathe. I stared dumbfounded for a few seconds before realizing what had happened. My mouth was open, but I could not speak. I was terrified and heard a thousand voices screaming in my mind. I threw the bag of peas into my backpack. I put on the bag as quickly as I could and ran. Why were they threatening to kill me? What crime had I committed? Did my attempt to find a place of emotional

refuge warrant capital punishment? Never mind all that. After what felt like an eternity, I stopped near an alleyway. I didn't remember how I had gotten there, and as I heard the passing cars and looked up at the crescent moon, my previous thoughts still burned in my mind. This was happening too often. Not being able to speak, I mean. I would have to find a new place to relax, and...overcome this incredible fear that left me crippled and hindered my ability to communicate.

Recognition Error

Short Story

I walked down the dark metal hallway, flipping a coin through my fingers to keep myself busy. The walls tilted when I leaned…it might have been my head, though. It'd been a long night. I finally came to my apartment. I felt like crud, looked like crud, and had barely any recollection of what I had done in the last five hours. My jeans were beat up and torn from that bar fight I had just been in, my shirt was stained, and I'm pretty sure I ripped my leather jacket. Even worse, every footstep left some dark, sticky print that I guessed was made of blood. I was too blitzed to care.

I punched my card to open the blast-proof door and walked over to my office. God, this place is a mess. *What happened here?* Someone had flipped over the desk and bookshelf. Papers were everywhere, and the drawers of the dresser were all open. I heard heavy breathing. It sounded animalistic, I think. I couldn't really think. I felt floaty, but thought I should feel afraid.

"Hey, Ronan, you here, dude? Someone's trashed the place." I heard no response. I started to snap out of my dreamlike state. I realized something was seriously wrong. I took out my pistol and held it at the ready before walking into the living room.

As soon as I stepped in, I realized I had a gun pointed at my head. I looked to Ronan, my roommate and lifelong best friend. He looked crazed. His hair was all frizzled up, his beard was unkempt, and his eyes looked bloodshot.

"R-ro, bud, what's this all about?" I said, dropping the gun and slowly raising my hands as adrenaline and anxiety began coursing through

my veins. Ronan and I were mercs, and I knew the look on his face. It was the same one he had when we were fighting our way through that complex on Sapphire Three. Something was seriously wrong.

He hit his head as if it were bothering him before talking in a low, angry voice. "Who are you?"

"Ronan? Dude, it's me. Jax. Your buddy. You been…you been using lately?"

"Using? Using…I don't touch anything, I don't think. Or do I? I …" He hit his head again in a sporadic motion. "I can't remember anything…Who did you say you were again?" He still had the gun pointed at me.

"Jax, dude. You know me."

"Like hell I know you. Get outta here before I put a hole in your chest."

I suddenly realized what was happening. I hoped this day would never come. There were many diseases cured by the second solari, but memory degradation wasn't one of them. I was looking at it now, just in front of me, both terrifying and terrified, wide-eyed and scatterbrained, alone. That was what it made you. And my friend Ronan, who I'd known longer than anybody, had succumbed to it.

"Ronan, listen." I said while backing away. "You're not thinking right. Let's just…let's head to the doctor, alright?"

"I don't know who you are, and I'm not interested in finding out. *Get outta here*!"

Here he was. The friend I left Luxfall with, the one I worked with for twelve years as a bounty hunter, the one who got me out of the citadel when the job on Virex Prime went south. I could still see the face that had such a beautiful smile when he told me about his first girlfriend, the eyes that would widen whenever someone mentioned donuts.

"Okay, dude. S-sorry about this. But…you should really get checked out. I don't think–"

I eyed my pistol on the floor as I said this, and he noticed. I didn't get a moment to react before he started shooting. I was hit in the arm and fell back. I was able to grab my gun from off the floor and was left with an impossible choice–save myself and risk killing the only person who cared whether or not I made it home, or die trying to reason with someone clearly not in their right mind. He once told me never to point a gun unless I was ready to kill.

My hand was warm on the handle.

He was ready to kill.

Was I?

I let go of the gun and turned to leave, clutching my bleeding arm all the way.

Episode 1: Introductions

Screenwriting Excerpt

GORO, a sentient, bipedal, genetically-modified gorilla, walks through the streets of New York, getting stares. He is wearing a blazer, button down shirt, and monocle. He reaches the apartment complex and enters. GORO anxiously checks his watch as he ascends the stairs. The apartment is dark and somewhat dingy. He is carrying a box with a few items in it– a laptop, some photographs, and books. He reaches the door of the apartment and rings the doorbell. Some rustling is heard inside the room before the door is opened by a futuristic humanoid robot, ROBO. ROBO doesn't move mechanically– it behaves like a human in its movement and even looks like it's tired, hungover, or sick. GORO did not expect this to be his roommate and looks somewhat surprised before attempting to greet the robot but acting awkwardly.

GORO
Hello. I am Goro. Is this apartment 471?

ROBO
[somewhat annoyed]
Yeah. I'm, uh, I'm Robo. You my new roommate?

GORO
I believe so, yes. May I come in?"

ROBO
Oh yeah, of course.

As GORO enters, he sees that the apartment is a mess. There are papers strewn everywhere and things are just left all about

(motor oil and different things all just put onto tables or thrown on the floor.) GORO is immediately irritated by this but because he is anxious does not show it through anger– it just seems like he is trying to control himself.

GORO
Where should I put my things?

ROBO
Uh, your room is in the back.

GORO awkwardly goes to his room, stumbling over the random items as he goes.

GORO (aside)
[mumbling]
Good God, how am I going to live like this? The robot is...and the apartment! It's a mess! This is… unacceptable. Completely unacceptable! But what did I expect? Of course they'd pair me with– no, no, it's fine. I'll manage. I always manage.

GORO sets up his things in his room. He then goes back out and looks for Robo.

GORO
Hey, uh, Robo? Why is the apartment in this condition?

ROBO
What condition? The mess? I just don't bother to clean up around here. I don't really even use any of the stuff that's here, but I just don't know where to put it.

GORO
Well, in that case, do you mind if I clean the apartment and you keep it the same way?

ROBO
[Surprised]
I—That sounds great, actually. Please do. I can help out, too.

GORO cleans the whole place compulsively while ROBO is taking a nap and then hands ROBO a paper with a comprehensive list and categorization of where everything is in the apartment now. This is meant to show a baseline of their dynamic— one trying to help the other both compulsively and because of genuine altruism.

Jaleah Parks

Jaleah Parks was born in Nashville, Tennessee, and is currently in high school. She enjoys designing and watching Netflix in her free time. Jaleah aspires to become an interior designer and finds writing to be a peaceful outlet that helps her express thoughts she may not feel comfortable saying out loud. She lives by the quote: "Don't try to write your story, let God write it for you."

Pain

Poetry

My heart is filled with pain.
Each day I wake up, and it's the same.
As I awake, I start to ache.
My heart fills with a raging pain,
As if I need to gain,
But somehow, all I feel is pain

Wake

Short Story

After Sandra escaped a toxic relationship, she made a vow to herself, promising to stay cautious of men and not get in too deep with them anymore—just have some fun with them. So she joined an app called FoundR, and she matched instantly. She went on a few dates, had a couple of drinks. Then she met Jim.

Sandra was very hesitant with Jim. Even though he seemed like a good guy, Sandra was still scared to move too fast. But it seemed like Jim wanted to move at a very fast pace in the relationship, so Sandra decided it was best to end the relationship , because it was starting to seem like Jim wanted something permanent, while Sandra was still afraid and just wanted "fun." So she broke it off.

Sandra texts Jim, "You're an amazing guy, but I think we should break things off as it is." Jim doesn't reply, so Sandra blocks him.

A couple days later, items inside Sandra's house were missing—important items. Later, she noticed his car outside her job, house, and gym. Sandra did the only logical thing: she went to the police station and filed a report on Jim. The officers began to gaslight Sandra, telling her that she was overthinking and sending her home.

Sandra was really triggered by the event, and even more on edge. As Sandra arrives back home, she discovered her front door wide open. Despite recognizing it would be a bad idea, she still walked right in, unaware that would be the worst decision of her life. As soon as she was through the door, it slammed shut, and someone grabbed her and covered her mouth before she could even scream. The grip felt familiar, and she realized it was Jim. She stopped

thrashing for a moment, and he hesitantly lifted his hand.

"What do you want from me, Jim? Let me go!"

Jim whispers in Sandra's ear, "You will never get away from me. We are meant to be together forever."

Sandra screamed and tried to fight back, but it was useless. Jim was way stronger than Sandra. He covered her mouth again, but she was not done yet. She kicked and screamed and flailed as Jim dragged her into his car trunk. He wrestled her shoes off so she couldn't kick him, then slammed the gate down and went to start the car.. She kept kicking and screaming, and while she made a good ruckus, Jim wouldn't let her try for long. He pulled over, opened the trunk, and arned her: "Shut up, or I will kill you." He then slams the trunk again.

Sandra couldn't believe that such a good guy could turn into something that she despised. She didn't know whether she would make it out of this alive or if she would die. She didn't know what lengths Jim would be willing to go to.

Every breath Sandra took felt like she was inhaling fear. Her heart beat so loudly, she was sure he could hear it from the driver's seat. Her wrists ached from struggling to get the zip ties off her hands. Her legs cramped in the tight space, but she didn't stop trying to push against the walls of the trunk, kicking at the taillights, praying something will give.

She stopped for a moment, tired and in despair, and she heard silence. The car was not moving anymore. She wonder: Has he stopped somewhere? Are there people around? If she screamed, would they hear her? Is he waiting outside to see if she screamed or made a noise?

She looked around in the trunk to see if there was anything she could use to try and open the trunk. She saw a screwdriver, but she couldn't seem to reach it. So she twisted and moved in mysterious directions to get closer to the screwdriver, and she managed to

reach it. She started trying to break the zip ties.

She heard heavy footsteps, and realized there was no time. The footsteps stopped directly in front of the trunk, and the trunk opened slowly.

"Don't make this harder than it needs to be," Jim said. His eyes were filled with hatred. "We are just going to talk, Sandra. I just want us to be together and have a happy life."

Sandra has no words except: "NO!"

Jim continued to try and talk to her, and Sandra continued to scream "NO." Jim grew impatient and forcefully tried to slam the trunk.

Sandra thought fast and yells, "*Wait*! Wait, we can talk."

Jim smiled. "Finally, you've come to your senses." He reached in to grab her, but she lunged up and stabbed Jim with the screwdriver.

He cursed, stumbled backward. For a split second, Sandra saw her chance. She scrambled out of the trunk, hit the ground hard, and took off running.

She didn't know where she was. It looked like the edge of the woods. There was a gravel road, no houses in sight, and it was nearly dark. But she ran until she couldn't possibly run anymore. Barefoot, she pushed through tree branches, not caring how they whipped against her skin.

Behind her, she heard him shout, "Sandra! Come back! You're making this worse! I will find you no matter what!"

She didn't stop.

Branches snagged her hair. A rock cut into her foot. Her lungs burned. But she kept running.

Finally, after what felt like forever, she saw a light– a house. Just one porch light on, dim in the distance.

She sprinted to what looked like the front door, banged on it with everything she had. "Help! Please! Someone help me!"

An older woman opened the door, startled. Her eyes widened when she saw Sandra, bleeding and shaking on her porch.

"Dear God, what happened?"

"He's coming... he kidnapped me... please call the police!"

The woman pulled her inside, locked the door, and grabbed the phone.

Sandra collapsed onto the floor, sobbing. She didn't even realize she was hyperventilating until the woman knelt next to her with a glass of water.

Within minutes, flashing red and blue lights flickered in the distance.

Once they arrived, she knew that everything was going to be okay.

Government Cuts Water Supply as Gruesome Discovery Surfaces

Story Excerpt

The taps didn't just slow— they stopped.

By dawn, the water had vanished from every faucet in town. No warning. No explanation. Just silence where there should have been flow.

In the first few hours, many assumed it was another drought-related issue. After all, the past few summers had brought water restrictions. But this felt different. And by noon, the truth began to leak— not from the pipes, but from the people.

The town's only remaining maintenance worker, speaking under anonymity, revealed that the government had shut off the town's main waterline manually. Not for repairs. Not for rationing. But for reasons classified and undisclosed, even to local officials.

That's when the fear began.

At an emergency town hall— where no water was served and the air reeked of panic —Mayor Carla Jennings stood stiffly behind the podium. Her voice was hoarse, her words clearly chosen.

"There has been… a situation in the water system. Federal agencies are involved. I ask for patience, for calm. I can't say more at this time."

But the truth couldn't be contained.

That evening, a whistleblower from the Environmental Testing Division leaked what many had feared: human remains had been discovered inside the town's reservoir.

Not one. Not two. Multiple bodies.

Preliminary reports suggested the remains had been decomposing for months, if not longer. The discovery was made during a routine pressure inspection. When a submersible drone went offline, a retrieval dive was ordered. Instead of equipment failure, divers found bones. Bones buried in the silt on the floor, tied with wire and industrial tape. Some wrapped in canvas. Some still wearing faded clothing.

As news spread, the question on everyone's lips wasn't just "Who are they?" but "Have we been drinking this?"

Federal biohazard teams arrived within hours. Hazmat suits replaced utility uniforms. Fences went up. Drones circled. And still, no official word.

Unofficially, speculation ran wild.

Some say the discovery was tied to the disappearance of migrant workers from a nearby development site last year– cases that had been quietly dismissed.

Others believe it's a cover-up of a long-forgotten crime ring operating through old government contracts in the region using the reservoir as a dumping ground.

And some, whispering more fearfully, believe it's connected to a secret government program – something darker, something deliberately erased.

Now, the town is left parched, and not just for water. For truth. For safety. For closure.

Children drink bottled water in schools. Showers are banned. Lawns are turning to dust. But the most corrosive drought is the one

beneath the surface: the trust lost between a town and the system meant to protect it.

What was once a simple crisis of supply has become something far more terrifying:

A mystery with bodies in the water.

And no one is willing to say how they really got there.

Shadows in the Quarter

Playwriting Excerpt

[Scene 1: New Orleans, 1920. The French Quarter. The stage is set with cobblestone streets, wrought-iron balconies, and flickering gas lamps. In the background, a faint echo of a jazz trumpet plays from somewhere unseen. Faded posters line the walls with words like "The River Knows," "Missing Since 1914," and "Fortune Telling Inside." The light is dusky, nearly evening.]

Curtains open slowly. Lights dim to simulate dusk. Fog curls in around the edges of the stage. BETHANY and BRITTANY enter stage right, walking with purpose, but tension between them is obvious. BETHANY is looking around and clutching an old letter in her hand.

BETHANY
The letter said he'd be near Royal Street. He used to frequent The Green Lily Café. That's where we'll start.

BRITTANY
sighs
You don't even know if this Adam guy exists, Bethany. You've got us chasing rumors. I should be home helping Mama.

BETHANY
[firmly, but weary]
And what help are you to her if we never find out what happened to Dad? She wakes up every night calling his name. I need answers. We need answers.

BRITTANY
[cynical]
You mean you need closure. Not me. Not like this.

BETHANY[
softly
You were too young to remember him leaving. I saw the way he looked at Mama the night before he disappeared. Like he knew. Like he wasn't coming back.

BRITTANY slows her pace. There's a long pause between them as they walk further into the Quarter. Street performers dance nearby, and a tarot reader watches them pass from her stoop.

BRITTANY
[tired]
What's this Adam supposed to be? A hero? A detective? You think he just has answers for strangers walking in off the street?

BETHANY
[under her breath]
I just know...

BRITTANY
[annoyed[
You always do that. Say things like that. "I just know." Like it's some sixth sense. Well, I don't know anything, and neither do you.

BETHANY
[sharply]
No time for the attitude, Brittany. Just stay close. This place changes after dark.

BRITTANY stops walking. Crosses her arms.

BRITTANY
[angry]
Maybe I don't want to stay close. Maybe I'm tired of following your wild goose chases through ghost-town streets. Maybe I want something real.

BETHANY stops too. For a moment, her expression softens. She's tired, stretched thin, but her voice stays calm.

BETHANY
[quietly]
I get it. I do. But if Dad is still out there—if Adam knows anything...I have to try. You can stay angry. Just don't get lost.

BRITTANY storms off stage left. BETHANY watches her go with regret, but she turns back to her path. She walks alone now. The atmosphere grows heavier. She begins to ask people as she moves.

BETHANY
Excuse me, sir—Adam Broussard. Know the name?

STREET VENDOR
[avoiding eye contact]
Don't know him. Don't want to.

BETHANY approaches the fotune teller.

BETHANY
Please... Adam. He was tied to a man named Louis. He used to work the river.

FORTUNE TELLER continues to stare into her cards, not looking up.

FORTUNE TELLER
Names like Adam don't belong in daylight. You're chasing shadows, girl.

BETHANY walks further downstage, muttering, almost losing hope.

BETHANY
[muttering to herself]
You were supposed to be here. You wrote me...

BETHANY pulls out the letter and reads it out loud.

BETHANY
"You want the truth? Come to the Quarter. Ask for me where the moon cuts through smoke." What does that even mean?

Suddenly, a man's voice calls from off-stage, raspy and slow.

ADAM
You ask too loud for a man that likes to stay forgotten.

BETHANY spins. The lights shift to a low amber glow. A shadow steps from an alleyway—a man in a dark coat and brimmed hat.

BETHANY
[(startled]
Are you Adam?

ADAM
[deep, gravelly]
That depends. Who's asking?

BETHANY
Bethany Lang. My father was Samuel Lang. You knew him. Or you knew something. He disappeared off the river six years ago.

ADAM studies her, long pause.

ADAM
I knew Sam. But knowing something… and telling it… that's a different thing entirely.

BETHANY
[desperate]

Please. We don't have time. My sister ran off. My mother's fading. I need something–anything. Why did you send me the letter?

ADAM doesn't answer immediately. The jazz trumpet from earlier begins to swell in volume. The lights flicker.

ADAM
Because your father didn't disappear.

(Beat. Silence hits the stage like thunder.)

BETHANY
[whispers]
Then where is he?

ADAM steps closer, lowers his voice.

ADAM
You want the truth? Then come with me. But know this–truth in this town doesn't come clean. And it doesn't come free.

BETHANY hesitates... then follows Adam slowly into the shadows. A silhouette of BRITTANY is seen far stage left, watching them go.

Lights dim to black. Jazz fades to silence.

[End Scene]

Andrea Reynolds

Andrea is from Nashville, Tennessee, and finds joy in fighting (for fun), watching anime, and getting plenty of rest. She will be attending Cumberland University and aspires to become an accomplished writer. Andrea enjoys writing fan fiction and is motivated by the quote: "Your actions define who you are."

School Shootings

Article Writing Excerpt, Formal

There are many problems in our modern school system. The major problems that I will cover in this article are bullying and cyberbullying, which in turn can lead to school shootings and student suicides. Solving these issues has proved difficult due to a lack of consensus on how to handle them among different groups. Everyone believes their way is best, and when differing ideas clash, solutions are stalled. However, students like myself can do several things to keep raising awareness and furthering solutions, such as organizing protests and sit-ins. The key is to keep organizing until we achieve results.

Dorian Rhodes

Dorian Rhodes was born in Knoxville, Tennessee, and raised in Nashville. He enjoys video games, playing and watching sports, and social studies. Dorian dreams of becoming an architect, making a lot of money, and eventually living in Texas. He writes fiction essays and strives to improve by overcoming procrastination. His strengths include being a strong visual learner. He hopes to attend Rice University and is guided by the advice: "Don't rush life—it's not as fun as it looks." His favorite quote: "Believe you can, and you're halfway there."

Adjust

Short Story

Life hasn't been easy since my accident. It's been over a year, and a major setback. I'm 16 now; being hand-fed hurt my pride. I'm better physically, but I don't know mentally. Since I was three, my dad has helped me realize my biggest dream. To hoop. I've worked too hard to let this accident take away long nights and early mornings of basketball. I don't remember a lot of things right now, but I do remember the impact of basketball on my life. School starts tomorrow, but I don't really know if I'm ready.

My alarm beeps. I stare at the ceiling. First day of school. My twin sister, Kaylee, comes into my room saying, "James, come down for breakfast!" I eat, get changed, and wait at the door for Kaylee. She comes down and we walk to the bus stop. She's been very protective of me since my accident. She's my best friend and is very emotional about everything that happened. As we get off, she emphasizes to me to take it easy. We go to get our schedule as people notice my return. My best friend, Jonathan, hugs me tightly.

"I can't believe it's you!" He saw me from time to time, but I was in a coma. My new schedule shows that I share first period with him and Kaylee, so I gingerly walk alongside them.

In the middle of the day, as I walk to lunch, I see the flyers. Basketball tryouts soon. I know what I'm doing August 27th-31st. Kaylee tries to convince me otherwise, but I drown all noise out. I hear it: *"Now starting at point guard, the return of number 0, James Hart!"* This was my comeback story. A legendary one at that. No one could convince me otherwise.

After long nights of wobbly legs, a tumble on some drives, iffy jumpers, and (an attempt of) re-finding my vertical, I began to feel good. It was now the 24th, about three weeks since the first day. I've been practicing since I was cleared out of the hospital. "I am ready," I repeat in my head. Three sleeps later, and it was the day. Tryouts day. I pack an extra bag, fill up a water bottle, pack my sneakers, and run out the door.

"Wait up! Hold on, James!" Kaylee shouts.

"Oh yeah, sorry, K. Just excited is all," I say with a chuckle.

While on the bus, Kaylee says, "I believe in you no matter what, James, but promise me you won't get hurt. Not just today in practice, but this season. I couldn't live to see you hurt again."

"Pinky swear," I say.

After a few hours, the clock strikes 2:00. It's time. Boys aged 14-18 walk towards the gym with anticipation. In the crowd, I find Jonathan, who is excited as well.

"Welcome back, man!" he says.

"The honor is mine," I say jokingly with a bow. Jonathan was never as bought-in to basketball as I was, but since we've been friends, it's kinda rubbed off on him. I mean, it probably would after eleven years, y'know? We put our bags in the locker room and get to stretching. After about five minutes, Coach Henry blows his whistle.

With a stern look on his face and Assistant Coach Parker next to him, he says, "Welcome, boys of Baxter-Carter High School. Some of you may know me, some of you may not. Some of you hate me already. Good. This won't be easy, and not all of you will make the team. Prove why I should let you on my team." Coach Parker splits us up into our groups. As I start to move, Coach Henry calls me over.

"Mr. Hart," he starts, "welcome back." Coach Henry was an older man with an old-school feel. Always serious, no funny business. "I just hope you know," he says, "just because you were a star doesn't mean I'll just let you on my team. Prove you still got it, kid." I nod. "Now go and get with your group." I walk away with a sigh.

We start with simple layups, a breeze. Jump shots, dribbling, sprints, free throws, passing– I do decent. I still need to be better. Then, groups pair for scrimmages.

We get paired with Aiden's group. Aiden hates my guts. He believes I stole his spot freshman year. He's gonna try to get "revenge" this year.

"Hope you're ready for the fireworks," he says, bumping my shoulder with a stupid grin. As scrimmages went on, I struggled against him. Missed shots, bad passes, loose balls, it felt like I couldn't do anything. I was already frustrated enough when Aiden said something that sent me over. "Maybe you should've stayed in the hospital, Hart," as he chuckles.

Game on. Cuts. Curves. Shots. Swish. He's asked for it. I've turned my game up a notch. I'm flying like the accident never happened. Breezing past defenders. Fade away shots and all. He's tired. Out of breath.

"Keep up next time, Williams," I tell Aiden.

Me, Kaylee, and Jonathan walk home together.

"So?" Kaylee asks.

"It was cool. Just coming back into it and all," I say, kind of staring off into the distance.

"Dude, what?" Jonathan starts, "You were killing it out there! You looked like 14-year-old James Hart, peak athleticism!" I sigh. I don't know what the next direction is. The truth is, none of that first day

was easy. It was tiring. The adrenaline in the moment lifted me. Now, my body has completely worn down. I walk with a limp until we get home.

"See y'all tomorrow," Jonathan says.

"See ya, J."

"James, come down for dinner!" Kaylee calls. We sit down next to each other and eat, but it feels a little tense.

"Are you okay?" I ask, breaking the silence.

"Yeah, just… thoughtful," she responds. "Are you sure this is all gonna work? That this isn't too… you know… sudden?" I take a little to respond. Is this too sudden? Maybe. Too late to turn back now.

"K, you're my twin sister, and my best friend. I don't keep secrets from you. I couldn't if I wanted to. Everything will work out. I promise." She gives me a weak smile. She isn't completely satisfied, but I guess it's better than nothing.

For the rest of the week, tryouts go on. I'm not who I once was, but I guess even post-accident me is one of the better players at this school. I've made the roster, but only under one condition, according to Coach Parker. They'll only let me play if I go to physical therapy. Kaylee also says I have to do this. I mean, might as well. It starts on Monday with Dr. Richards; not really excited about it, but I probably do need it.

Monday comes fast, and after long hours of school, I go to practice. Jonathan made the team— I'll admit, I don't quite know how, but he did.

"Dude, we're gonna be like D. Wade and LeBron!"

I jokingly roll my eyes. "More like Batman and Robin," I say back.

"Whatever, man." We laugh as we open the gym doors. Practice goes as usual. Shots go up. Defensive drills. You get the picture.

Kaylee stands, dangling her keys. "Physical therapy!" I sigh. "You pinky swore, remember? You can never break a pinky swear," Kaylee says.

"You're right."

At physical therapy, Dr. Richards asks me a string of questions. "What caused you're limitations on the physical abilities you once had?" I immediately have a flashback.

January 22nd, 2024

"*Now, you're Carter-Baxter Fightin' Tigers! …Now, starting at point guard, number zero, Jaaaaamessss Hart!" The crowd cheers. James runs out onto the court. Does his handshake with Jonathan. He lines up in the backcourt for tipoff. Here we go. Halfway through the 3rd and it's 57-48. Hart has 36. He's cooking the Terrence Rose Cardinals tonight. Slicing through the D, cut to the basket, step back three. They can't stop him. With 3:29 left on the clock and 10 seconds left on the shot clock, it's time to make a play. At the top of the key, he calls for a screen. Screen received. He rolls around the screen. Dribble. Dribble. Cuts towards the basket. Shot clock reads 7… 6… James takes flight. He goes for the layup. The center cuts in to stop James, but he's already in the air. The ball leaves his hand. Nowhere to land. The ball goes in. James is hit from the side. He freefalls toward the ground, bracing for impact. He topples over. Head first. To the ground. Boom. The ref blows the whistle for the basket and the foul. But James is down. He's not getting up. Kaylee lets out a huge scream. He's not moving. They bring out a stretcher and load him onto the ambulance. All a blur for James. Only Kaylee*

and everyone around him remembers.

After physical therapy, I hope in the car with Kaylee. Before starting the car, she says, "So, how was it?"

"Cool, I guess," I respond.

"Well, it better be great soon." I laugh after she says that. It felt good. I haven't really laughed a lot recently. She turns the radio onto 94.5, our favorite radio station. "Party in the USA" comes on, and we sing along. She stops at McDonald's before we get home. We eat and get ready for bed. "Night, James."

"Night, K." I sleep, knowing I'll be playing a competitive basketball game soon.

The week comes and goes. Friday night. The Hyatt County Wranglers are coming to our arena. After school, Jonathan and I grab our bags and head to the gym.

"The man is back!" he says excitedly.

"Calm down, man," I say with a laugh. "Let's take it one game at a time. I'm back when I score 30 again." The locker room is buzzing with anticipation when Coach Henry walks in. He gives the normal pregame speech.

"Boys, this is it. I've trusted you enough to represent me and this school on that court. Prove me right and represent this school right. The starting lineup for today…" He starts going through the list, but all I want to know is point guard. Finally: "…and at point guard will be James Hart. Go out and get ready for warmups."

It was when he said my name that I realized I'd been holding my breath. I let out a huge sigh of relief. We get into layup lines and do warmups. During warmups, Coach Parker pulls me aside.

"James, just know, we don't need you to be Superman. We understand what happened the last time you played a basketball game. If things are shaky, we'll put you on a minutes restriction. We care about you and your health. Let's go win a basketball game."

Before going back, I see Kaylee. I go to her, do our handshake, and give her a hug. She's my biggest supporter. "Be great, James!" she says.

After warmups, I make sure everything is right. Shoes tied. I tuck my jersey into my shorts. Arm sleeve on. I sit on the bench, thinking. I zone out during pregame introductions until I snap out, hearing: "And now, the return of your starting point guard, number 0, James Hart!" I jump off the bench and run up and give all my teammates high fives, including my special handshake with Jonathan.

I line up in the backcourt and get ready for tipoff. The ref blows his whistle. Game time. We win the tip, and the crowd goes crazy.

I get the ball in my hand, and for a second, the whole world felt light. Like I was floating. I call the play, and we get the game started. I'm not letting this comeback game be an 'okay' one. I'm letting it be one for the ages. No minutes restriction. I'm going hard. Assists. Cuts towards the basket. Step back shots. Spin to the basket. I'm playing the best defense I've played in my life.

By the 4th, I check back into the game with 34 points, 7 assists, 2 rebounds, and 1 steal. I'm ready to go again. I'm at the top of the key dribbling. 10 seconds left on the shot clock. I call for a screen. Screen received. I roll around the screen. Dribble. Dribble. I cut toward the basket. Shot clock reads 7… 6… I take flight. I go for the layup. The center cuts in to stop me, but I'm already in the air. The ball leaves my hand. Nowhere to land. The ball goes in. I'm hit from the side. Then I fall.

Rent-Free

Playwriting

[Scene 1: Inside of a cramped apartment in New York. Pizza boxes stacked up. A laptop open with spreadsheets. One corner has a coat rack with a fake wig and sunglasses on it. A door to the hallway, and three bedroom doors. It's early morning.]

MAYA is on her laptop. JAY is lying on the couch. RILEY is finger painting on a cereal box. TINA enters and waves a mail envelope.

TINA
Mail's here. It's from the landlord.

JAY
Maybe it's a love letter. He's always complimenting my mustache. *chuckles*

TINA
You don't have a mustache.

JAY
Not right now.

RILEY
[not looking up]
If it's another rent hike, I'm starting a rent hike in the living room. First meeting will be shirt optional.

MAYA stands, takes the letter, and opens it.

MAYA
I knew it! I *knew* it! Rent's going up $500 a month.

OTHERS
WHAT?!

JAY
Okay. Chill. That's, like, only… *tries math, fails* a lot of money.

TINA
We already split rent four ways. We can't afford another increase.

All sit in heavy silence, thinking.

RILEY]
What if…

OTHERS
What?

RILEY
Never mind.

All go back to thinking.

RILEY
But what if…

OTHERS
Yes??

RILEY
No that's stupid.

OTHERS
[groaning]
Riley!

RILEY
I GOT IT!

OTHERS
What???

RILEY

What if… and hear me out… we add a fifth roommate?

JAY
To our two-bed apartment?

RILEY
Not a real one… an imaginary one.

TINA
You're suggesting we lie. To our landlord.

MAYA]
Wait. Wait wait wait wait wait. That's… not a bad idea.

RILEY
Thank you.

MAYA
If we "add" a fifth roommate, divide rent five ways… we each pay less than we do now. Even with the increase.

JAY
We just need to make them believable. What should we name them?

MAYA
How about… Alex?

JAY
That's good. Gender neutral. Mysterious. Doesn't like people. Never leaves their room. Definitely allergic to daylight

TINA
This is extremely unethical.

RILEY
So is charging $2300 for a glorified shoebox

MAYA
Look, if we can just get through the next six months—

There is a loud knock at the door. All freeze.

JAY
Don't answer it! Maybe it's Alex!

[End Scene]

[Scene 2: Same living room, group in chaos. They pull together wigs, sunglasses, a trench coat, and print a fake lease. RILEY is taping a "DO NOT ENTER" sign on "Alex's" door. JAY is practicing a mysterious voice. MAYA is creating a fake social media page. TINA is holding her head in disbelief.]

JAY
[trying voices] "I am Alex." [deeper] "I… AM ALEX."

MAYA
Okay, Alex is now 29, works as a freelance data archivist, which I made up, but sounds boring and real.

RILEY
Also allergic to air freshener. So if he doesn't show up for inspections, it's "safety reasons."

TINA
What are we doing. What are we actually doing right now.

JAY
We're fighting back. Against The System.

TINA
We are committing fraud.

RILEY draws a mustache on JAY with a marker.

RILEY
Now it's performance art.

JAY
[serious]
Question. What Alex's backstory?

MAYA
Backstory?

JAY
People ask questions. I need to be Alex. *turns dramatically* Where is Alex from? What were his dreams before… the darkness?

RILEY
He's from Albuquerque. He once loved puppets. Now he fears them.

JAY
nods
That tracks.

TINA
We're going to jail.

MAYA
Nobody's going to jail, Tina. We're saving money.

Knock at the door. Everyone freezes again.

MAYA
Okay, okay. Deep breath. Nobody panic.

JAY grabs trench coat and sunglasses.

JAY
It's time.

TINA
No! Don't open the door in costume!

RILEY
We've come too far.

JAY dramatically opens the door to reveal… the pizza delivery guy.

DELIVERY GUY
Large mushroom, no cheese?

Everyone takes a deep sigh of relief, JAY takes the pizza.

JAY
Thank you, normal citizen. From one underpaid worker to another, keep fighting.

DELIVERY GUY
Sounds… good…?

DELIVERY GUY leaves. JAY shuts the door. Silence.

TINA
We've lost our minds.

RILEY
Nah. We've finally snapped into sync.

[End Scene]

[SCENE 3: Two days later. The apartment is suspiciously tidy. There's now a photo of "Alex" taped to the fridge (a blurry shot of JAY in sunglasses, mid sneeze). A bag of chips labeled "Alex's, DO NOT TOUCH" sits untouched. The group gathers nervously. MAYA enters holding her phone.

MAYA
Uhhh, guys. Emergency. Mr. Halpern is coming by tomorrow.

JAY
Did he say why?

MAYA

"Routine occupancy verification."

TINA
Which is landlord code for: "I already suspect you're lying."

RILEY
munching Alex's chips
So… it's showtime?

MAYA
No. We can't just present Alex like a high school science project. He needs to be felt, not seen.

JAY
You want me to haunt the apartment?

RILEY
Like Casper but rent conscious.

TINA
sighs, then stands
Okay. Fine. We fake the meeting. Alex's "job" suddenly requires an urgent travel. We leave signs. Suitcases. Noise machine playing "airport ambiance." Someone FaceTimes in as Alex from a fake airport background.

Silence

MAYA
…Tina?

RILEY
Did you just…?

JAY
FINALLY! You've joined the dark side.

TINA

shrugging
If we're lying, we're gonna do it right.

Everyone erupts into celebratory chaos. MAYA grabs her laptop, JAY pulls out the trench coat, RILEY starts filming background airport footage on their phone.

JAY
I'm so proud of her. It's like watching a deer pick up a sword.

[End Scene]

[Scene 4: The next day. Lights dim. Music playing soft "airport sounds." Suitcase by the door. Laptop open on a table with Alex's "FaceTime" ready. MAYA is seated next to the laptop. RILEY pretending to bake Alex's "favorite muffins." TINA trying to stay calm.

HALPERN knocks on the door.

MAYA
This is it. Everyone act natural.

She opens the door. Enter Mr. Halpern, clipboard in hand, already suspicious.

HALPERN
Afternoon. Just checking in. Quick headcount.

MAYA
Of course! There's me, Maya *nervous chuckle*, that's Riley in the kitchen, Jay, and Tina.

All smile awkwardly.

HALPERN
And…?

TINA
[perky]

Alex! He just left for a work conference in… *checks phone* Detroit. Very last minute.

HALPERN
Mmm. Shame. I've never seen him.

RILEY
He's deeply private. We all have a theory he's in witness protection.

MAYA gestures to laptop.

MAYA
But we can FaceTime him!

(She turns the laptop to Halpern. JAY appears in sunglasses, blurry, with an airport filter and loud jet sounds)

JAY/"ALEX"
Sup. Can't talk long. Flight delayed. WiFi trash. Go Yankees.

HALPERN
[squinting]
You look familiar…

JAY/"ALEX"
Everyone says that. It's the cheekbones. Okay, boarding now. Love you roommates, bye.

Call ends abruptly.

HALPERN
Right… Well… I'll just… take note of that. Everything seems to be… in order.

He steps out, still unsure.

JAY
Go Yankees…?

TINA
You panicked.

RILEY
I don't know. I kinda liked the chaos.

[End Scene]

Not the Full Story: Do School Grades Really Show What's Going On in the Classroom?

Article Writing, Formal

Everything in school seems to lead to one thing: the report card. Each letter grade is supposed to show how well a student performed in a class, with 'A' being the best and 'F' the worst. But do those letters really tell the full story? A lot of people judge students based on their grades, but is that fair? Do grades truly reflect who someone is as a learner, or is there more going on behind the scenes?

Inside classrooms all over the world, learning takes place every day. At every stage of life, we take tests to prove what we've learned over a certain period. Since tests usually make up the majority of a student's grade, they're treated as extremely important. But not all students do well on tests, and that doesn't necessarily mean they're bad students.

For starters, not every student is a strong test taker. Many educators, including Mrs. Myles of Middle Tennessee State University, have seen this firsthand. She explains that some students participate well, understand the material, and contribute meaningfully in class, but still struggle with tests. Whether it's anxiety, difficulty retaining information, or the way the test is formatted, some students simply don't do well in testing situations.

To address this, Mrs. Myles has introduced systems where students can earn back points after a test by summarizing their work or demonstrating their understanding in other ways. However, not all teachers provide this kind of flexibility. As a result, students who grasp the content may still end up with poor grades, simply because their strengths aren't reflected in traditional assessments.

Another major factor is the teaching itself. In order to learn, students need to be taught, and not all teachers are the same. Some may struggle with communication, lack consistency in expectations, or fail to provide the support students need to succeed. I personally remember an experience in 8th grade where my science group submitted the same project. The teacher accused us of plagiarism and gave us a zero, until my parents got involved, and the grade was changed to 100. That situation showed me how much influence a teacher has over a student's grade, and how that power can sometimes be misused or misunderstood. Of course, students also have a responsibility to stay focused and try their best, but it's not fair to place all the blame on them when the environment isn't always balanced.

A student's home life also plays a major role in academic performance. Some students face challenges outside of school, like caring for siblings, dealing with absent parents, or living in difficult financial conditions. Not everyone has the privilege of a calm, supportive home life. That kind of stress often carries over into the classroom. And while these challenges may not appear on a test or assignment, they can still have a serious impact on performance. This factor is difficult to argue against, because it's real and it affects students deeply.

So, do school grades really show what's going on in the classroom? In many cases, the answer is 'no'. It's not a simple issue. Students come from different backgrounds, face different challenges, and experience different teaching styles, which all influence their grades. That's why no one should be judged solely based on a letter or a number. Grades don't define a student's intelligence, effort, or

potential.

What really matters is growth, persistence, and the willingness to improve. A grade can rise. A situation can change. With support and determination, every student has the ability to move forward, no matter what their report card says. Adults, encourage your students, and the grades will only climb higher.

Alayna Tucker

Alayna Tucker is a driven and ambitious young woman from East Nashville with big dreams for the future. Though she's still exploring her college options, she's confident in her passion for the medical field, with interests in women's health and dentistry. Alayna hopes to one day own a home and create a life she loves in a vibrant city. Outside of her academic goals, she enjoys playing volleyball and dreams of traveling the world—especially to Italy or Greece. Her heart is set on the excitement and energy of city life, where she envisions building her future.

Burned Youth

Poetry

When we're young, we're taught to hold our tongue, for some, this includes staying silent even when stung, but it's that silence that burns the lungs.

Scorching flames, yet we're the ones to blame. On the inside, we're hollow, but it's from the knives that we swallow.

Oftentimes, we wish to release the screams, but we can't, so instead they remain gut-wrenching dreams.

We started as delicate flowers, but now we're weeds, Drained. Stripped of all power.

Ronnie Turner

Ronnie Turner is a 14-year-old scholar from Tennessee. Fascinated by astronomy, Ronnie also enjoys reading and participating in band. He aspires to become an astronomer and one day earn the Nobel Peace Prize. Ronnie enjoys writing both poetry and fiction and dreams of attending Princeton University. He believes in using knowledge across disciplines and is guided by the phrase: "Never guess, always know." He hopes to live in Denver, Colorado, and cares deeply about world peace.

When Dreams Bleed Reality

Short Story

Jake gasped for air as he awoke from a horrid dream, astonished and confused. "I've never had these dreams before," he muttered. He crept downstairs as if he had seen a ghost—or perhaps he had; who could tell? He retrieved a glass from the cabinet and slowly filled it with water, standing there in a state of shock, afraid to move, to think, even to go back to sleep. After finishing the water, he went to the bathroom, watching his chest rise and fall as he took slow, deep breaths. "I should try and head to bed," he thought, and so he did.

On Monday at 9:00 AM, Jake was filled with trepidation. As he struggled to get out of bed, he contemplated calling a therapist. First, he called his mother to tell her what had happened. "He-hello," he stammered.

"What's wrong, dear?" his mother asked. Jake cleared his throat as if he had a frog stuck there.

"I…I had a horrible dream," he choked out, suddenly dissolving into tears. A loud thud came through the phone.

His mother, concerned and distraught, yelled in a scared tone, "Stay with me; I'm on my way." She quickly arrived to find him lying unconscious on the ground. As fast as possible, she called 911, and he was admitted to the hospital.

"Mr. Morano, can you hear me?" the doctor asked.

"Ye-Yes, I can," Jake replied weakly. Suddenly, his mother burst through the hospital room door, anxious.

"Oh my gosh, honey, are you okay?" "

Yes, Mom, I'm fine, but I've been meaning to tell you, I–I had a bad dream."

His mother, astonished and worried, asked, "What was it?"

"Well, it's about Dad..." Jake said shakily. Ms. Morano sat there, scared, reminded of the old memories that brought terror into her life.

"W-Well, go ahead," she urged.

Jake replied, "The next thing to come out of my mouth is going to sound horrible, and it truly is. Dad was always a drug addict and an alcoholic, but he is dead now, I know. But here is the thing: in my dream, he was alive and armed. He came to your house to get 'revenge,' as he called it. He said you were a horrible wife, and his last and final 'mission' was to kill you. So, he did. I was too late. He barged through the door and pushed you down, then boom. All I heard was a gunshot, straight in your head. I saw you lying on the ground with blood rushing down your face. I screamed and cried, and that's when I woke up."

"Oh, honey," his mother said, "I will be okay. He is not here to hurt us anymore. We are safe, and that is all that matters. I love you, always remember that."

"I love you too, Mama," Jake expressed softly.

On Wednesday at 10:00 AM, Jake was waiting for his discharge papers. His mother returned from the restroom, excited to leave the hospital.

"Finally, we get to leave. It felt as if we were in a matrix," she said,

relieved.

"Yeah, Mama, I'm excited too. I have been wanting to get out of here and see a therapist ASAP," Jake replied. As Jake stood talking, a sudden knock caught his attention. Rap. Rap. Rap. "

Mr. Morano, here are your discharge papers. If you have any questions, feel free to ask," his doctor said.

Jake looked at him and said, "Uhm, no sir, I have no questions."

"Okay then, have a good day," his doctor said as he exited the room.

Jake and his mother packed up and prepared to leave. As soon as Jake's feet touched the ground outside, he exclaimed, "I'M FINALLY FREE AGAIN!" All his mother could do was laugh and call him silly. They got into the car and drove away from the hospital.

Later that day, Jake was home alone. He thought about his dream again and decided he should call a therapist. He picked up his phone and dialed the number. Beep. Beep. Beep.

"Hello, Wellsbury Therapists' Office, how may I help you?"

"Uh-Uh-Uh," Jake stuttered, "I would like to schedule an appointment."

"Ah, yes, we can do that. Dr. Samantha Smith has an opening tomorrow at 12:00 PM. Is that okay?" The receptionist asked.

"Oh yes, that will work for me," Jake replied.

"We will collect your information at the desk tomorrow, so please make sure to be 30 minutes early."

"Will do," Jake said steadily.

He hung up, the phone feeling cold against his ear, and a surprising sense of relief settled over him. "Tomorrow," he whispered to the empty room, "I start." He was not expecting miracles, but the prospect of discussing the awful nightmares felt like a beacon in

the darkness. He spent the evening idly flipping through television channels, but nothing held his interest. He attempted to read a mystery novel, but the words were blurred. His mind kept reverting to his father's menacing face, the glint of the weapon, and the sickening sound of his mother falling. He vigorously shook his head, attempting to dislodge the thoughts. "Stop it," he muttered, running a hand through his hair. "You're safe now. She's safe." He repeated this mantra until he felt calm enough to consider sleep.

The next morning, Jake arrived at the therapist's office forty-five minutes early. The morning air was cool. The office was in a residential house on a quiet, tree-lined street. The receptionist was pleasant and offered him a smile. "Good morning, Mr. Morano," she said softly. "Dr. Smith will be with you soon. Please sit down and relax."

He settled into a comfortable chair in the waiting room and tried to read a magazine, but his gaze continuously drifted to the clock. His heart raced, a mixture of apprehension about revisiting the past and hope that he was finally taking a step toward recovery. Dr. Smith called his name, her voice calm. "Jake? Come in."

Her office was bright and pleasantly scented, with notes of lavender and old books. Sunlight streamed through a large window. Dr. Smith was a kind woman; she gestured toward a chair. "Sit down, Jake," she said. "Take your time. Just tell me what is going on."

Jake sank into the chair. He took a deep breath and began recounting the dream, describing his father's return, the gunshot, and his mother on the ground. As he spoke, he felt a gradual alleviation, as if a heavy weight were being lifted. Dr. Smith listened without interruption, nodding and conveying understanding.

When he finished, the room was quiet, save for the hum of the air conditioning. Jake felt tired but also relieved. "Thank you for telling me that, Jake," Dr. Smith said softly. "That sounds truly scary. Dreams can be powerful; they often reflect our fears and sometimes resurface old traumas."

Jake nodded, feeling a glimmer of hope. He was not crazy after all.

“We’ll work on this together,” Dr. Smith said. “We’ll discuss your feelings and memories, and I’ll help you learn coping mechanisms. We can’t erase the dream, but we can strive to understand it, process emotions, and help you feel safe again.”

When Jake left the office, the world outside seemed a bit brighter, the air fresher. He knew the journey would be challenging, but he felt he finally had a chance. The dream had indeed wounded him, but now, with support, he had an opportunity to find peace once more.

From Roaring Twenties to Global Collapse: Understanding the Great Depression

Article Writing, Formal

The Great Depression, a crushing economic collapse that froze the world in the 1930s, is a sobering reminder of the fragility of modern economies and the magnitude of the human cost of massive economic catastrophe. Having started in America with the infamous stock market crash of October 29, 1929, also known as "Black Tuesday," its origins soon spread across the globe, presiding over a decade of unparalleled suffering, unemployment, and social upheaval.

Roots of the Catastrophe: A Fragile Prosperity

To understand the Great Depression, one must first look at the seemingly booming preceding decade: the "Roaring Twenties." While it was defined by technological advances, mass production, and a roaring stock market, this success lay on shaky ground. Speculative buying dominated, with nearly every individual and institution buying stocks on margin —borrowing amounts to purchase them. This inflated an artificial bubble, way more than the underlying firms' actual value.

Post-World War I agricultural overproduction caused falling crop prices, leaving farmers struggling with foreclosure and debt. Greater

income inequality was an issue as well, because very few people in their communities had money, resulting above the overall consumer demand. Secondly, many small banks went unregulated with weak banking systems and no resistance to panics. World trade deficits, war debt, and protectionism, like the Smoot-Hawley Tariff Act of 1930, and sharply raising import tariffs, fed the world economic depression by suppressing trade and retaliatory tariffs abroad.

The Crash and Aftermath: A Domino Effect

Black Tuesday was not the beginning, but the dramatic impetus that accelerated a chain reaction. When the stock prices fell, investors lost millions, and panic erupted. Banks, which were so keen on the stock market and subject to huge withdrawals by frightened depositors, underwent huge collapses. Having no federal insurance for deposits, people saw their life savings erased, leading to a fatal crisis of confidence in the banking system.

Firms, not able to obtain credit and with sales plummeting at the consumer level, cut back production and dismissed workers. Millions lost their jobs, a then-record 25% by 1933 in the United States, and millions more were underemployed. Families were evicted from their homes, famine ensued, and shantytowns—derisively named "Hoovervilles" after President Herbert Hoover—erupted nationwide. The social toll was monstrous, and mass despair and desperation permeated society.

Global Influence: A World Crisis

The Great Depression did not stay limited to the shores of America. Global interdependence of the world economy ensured that the crisis would spread worldwide in no time. The banks of America had borrowed from European nations, and in particular Germany and Austria, which were already burdened with war reparations and economic meltdown. Bank failures and economic meltdown followed in Europe. Exporting countries of raw materials, including those from Latin America and Asia, were also faced with dwindling demand for their exports, worsening each country's

respective crisis. The global gold standard monetary system, wherein currencies were pegged against a fixed amount of gold, also helped spread the crisis since nations deflated their economies to maintain their gold reserves.

Responses to the Crisis: From Laissez-Faire to the New Deal

Initial reactions to the Depression were rather inadequate. President Hoover, who was a proponent of minimal government intervention, held on to the principle of "rugged individualism" and resisted attempts at massive federal relief programs. He believed that the marketplace would self-correct and that private charities and local governments would take care of most of the crisis. Although he did sign some programs, like the Reconstruction Finance Corporation, to provide loans to industries and banks, they arrived too late and were too small.

Franklin D. Roosevelt's 1932 presidential election was a dramatic shift in government policy. Roosevelt, with his guarantee of a "New Deal" for Americans, set out on a series of full-scale programs designed to provide relief, recovery, and reform. The New Deal encompassed a very diverse range of policies:

- Relief: Initiatives such as the Civilian Conservation Corps (CCC) and Works Progress Administration (WPA) employed millions of individuals to construct infrastructure and public works facilities. The Federal Emergency Relief Administration (FERA) gave direct financial aid to the unemployed.
- Recovery: Stimulative measures were introduced in the economic front with the Agricultural Adjustment Act (AAA) for agriculturalists and the National Recovery Administration (NRA) in coming up with codes of fair competition (though the NRA later turned out to be unconstitutional).

- Reform: Radical long-term reform was attempted in order to prevent future depressions. The Glass-Steagall Act divorced commercial banking from investment banking, and the Federal Deposit Insurance Corporation (FDIC) was established to insure the money of depositors. The Social Security Act of 1935 created a national system of unemployment insurance, old-age pensions, and aid to dependent children and mothers that provided the foundation of the modern American welfare state. The Securities and Exchange Commission was created to regulate the stock market and prevent speculative excesses.

While the New Deal did not completely eliminate the Depression from the nation —it was the tremendous spending and war mobilization of World War II that actually brought the world economy out of the depths —it drastically cut back on suffering, restored optimism, and redefined for all time the function of government in American life.

Depression Legacy: A Shaped World

The Great Depression left its mark upon the world. It led to a wholesale reconsideration of economic theory, and John Maynard Keynes's reflections on the government intervention to boost demand were prominent. It prompted the growth of trade unions, where labor demanded more security and equal pay. Politically, it resulted in the development of extremist philosophies in many parts of the world, but in democratic countries, it helped instill the need for social security blankets on the part of the government and of government involvement in economic stability as well as society.

The Great Depression also created a growing fear of economic collapse that influenced policy formulation in the subsequent decades. It led to the establishment of global institutions like the International Monetary Fund (IMF) and the World Bank after World War II to provide international economic stability and prevent such an event.

In total, the Great Depression was a time of unashamed suffering and revolutionary change. It exposed the vulnerabilities of an unrestrained capitalist system and prompted governments worldwide to respond more interventional to protect their citizens and stabilize economies. Its lessons are still pertinent to us today, reminding us that sound economic policy, robust social safety nets, and the true need for global cooperation in a more globalized world matter.

Tsurah Waire

Tsurah Waire (pronounced Suh-Rawh Where) is a multidisciplinary creative who loves making just about everything—doodling, writing, crocheting, sewing, and even composing silly songs. A lifelong writer, Tsurah began with a mini-series called Sun's Adventure in elementary school and continued exploring poetry and storytelling through middle school and beyond. A graduate of Nashville School of the Arts, where she focused on literary arts, she dreams of one day impacting the world so deeply that museums might seek her journals after she's gone. Though she remains her own toughest critic, Tsurah embraces the beauty of creative expression and the journey of finding confidence through it.

Space Cats

Short Story

Nobody knows when, or why, cats started to walk on the highways to space. Scientists have been studying this catastrophic phenomenon for a few years now. Still no answer, no explanation, no reasoning. Nothing.

The highway to space, at first, was only for the rich. Kept away from the poor in chosen, secluded areas. Eventually, though, the poor wanted to drive to space too, but the government wasn't open to the idea. So, the poor decided to put the power into their own hands and fought for their rights to drive into space. To see all the stars and comets, all from the seats of their cars.

It took a while, but eventually all the fighting and all the protests wore the government out. About a year or so later, more highways and roads to space were built, open for everyone. Keeping everybody happy with their roads to space.

Recently, though, there have been rumors floating around amongst the poor.

"I heard that the rich paid construction workers to sprinkle cat food onto the highway's asphalt so that the roads would be full of cats, that way poor people wouldn't be able to use the roads," claimed 31-year-old Fred Demand.

The rumor would make more sense if it were accurate. The cats aren't just walking in the middle of the road. Oh no, not at all. They aren't savage animals! No, they walk in uniform, one single file line onto the highways leading to space.

Due to space lacking air, the cats used to freeze and float dead in space. The sight of tons of dead cats in space is not the prettiest sight. Especially not for the kids who come to see stars and planets. This led to the development of "S.T.E.C Star" workers, S.T.E.C standing for Stick Together Equipping Cats. They stand at the gate entry of each highway, suiting up every cat and kitten in a quick two-step cat space suit.

There are a few highways to space that haven't been fully built, so there are a few highways in space that have an entrance but not an exit leading back to Earth. Most cats walk on the finished highways, and it's preferred by most people, honestly. For at the end of every highway are newly built daycares for cats to (hopefully) be picked up by their owners. Most owners do give up on their cats, thinking that they're forever roaming the highways in space.

The cats that don't take the completed space highways are usually stuck floating with the stars forever. When kids are on Earth, they don't only watch the sky for shooting stars, but for "shooting cats" as well.

"First time I seen a shooting cat I had wisheded Miles [her cat] to come back from space, and then my Miles DID COME BACK!" said 6-year-old Layla D.

Unlike the well-known shooting star, after a "shooting cat" passes, a silhouette of a cat's head with ears shines through in the sky. Just for a split second.

Although scientists still can't find the cause for cats walking on these highways to space, they do predict that by 3082, cats will pollute almost 2% of Earth's orbit. With dead cats floating in space, it would make things more difficult for astronomers to study space as they do now. Maybe the government or scientists will make some sort of vacuum to remove all the cats from our orbit before things become polluted.

Rylan Wetsell

Rylan Wetsell is a passionate reader and writer from Nashville, Tennessee. He proudly identifies as a conlanger and internet swashbuckler. Rylan dreams of becoming a world-renowned scientist and author. For now, he enjoys life with his two dogs and close-knit family. He lives by Randall Munroe's quote: "If at first you don't succeed, that's one data point."

Pictures of a Leaf

Poetry

You talk about the leaf like it is the thing that it was
You describe how it stood so mighty on the tree
You describe its great fall like the fall of the Roman Empire
And its final rest like the resting of the dead
But this is not the leaf

The leaf is not the place where it stood
It is nothing of its height, or the wind that shook it
Do you see it there? Its graceful folds
Its thin lines and its elegant form
I pick up the leaf

See? The leaf is still the same as it is
Only a tremor, so slight, runs through it
Its past has changed it, sure
So its future will turn it to lines and dust
But the leaf stands the same

So while you think of the leaf, and the past and its fate
Now it stands there still, but its stand does not matter
Only, will you look! Will you admire its shape!
But no, you prattle on about what this leaf means
But this is not the leaf

Empty Page

Poetry

I want to stare a while
At an empty page that begs
To be filled with thoughts

Acrostic (A Poem in Too Few Lines)

Poetry

A million words, yet
Confined, compared to the
Racing of the thoughts
Or maybe
Structured, this conformity is
Torture, yet all I can express
Inside these lines cannot
Contain what is within me

The Nightmares are Never Gone

Short Story

Elian stepped through the house like a pile of glass jars. He wanted to run, to feel the sweet release as soon as possible, but Imira was home, and the last thing he wanted her to see was his desperation. His vision tunneled, narrowing on the doorway and the drawer, the one that held his box of dreamsticks. He stuffed one hand inside his pocket to keep it from shaking, but it continued despite his protests. He was thankful, at least, that his legs didn't give out. He let out a gasp. Inside his thoughts, the clawing of the demons began anew, their wailing and screeching growing more and more intense. Oh, that horrible screeching! Was it the cry of his own despair? The rage and cruelty of the creatures themselves? Perhaps, as he dreaded, it was some kind of sick joy. Some depraved jubilee that grew more ecstatic at each new depth of his suffering.

Before he knew it, he was at the drawer, fumbling with the lock. The key dropped from his hands. He cursed and picked it up, focusing just enough to fit the key into the lock and turn it until it clicked. He yanked the door open with undeserved violence and grasped at the box, picking up one of the dreamsticks. He had barely lit the stick with the tinderbox before it was in his mouth. He breathed deeply, letting the smoke wash away the screams, calm the storm of mental blood and bile that burned in his skull. *It's just memories,* he thought, *and they can't hurt you now.* Indeed, the Horrors seemed so much more distant now. With each breath, the buzzing in his mind calmed.

Elian checked the box; only four left. He was using them more and more often, and he'd purchased a higher dosage too. He wasn't

sure if it was the drug itself or if the Horrors were getting worse, but either way, it was worrying. He'd seen what happened to people who got lost in smoking dream, and he knew he would have to be careful, even if it was helping him manage the Horrors. But between his family dealing with a mumbling invalid and a death-bound, violent psychopath, there were no good options.

His wife Imira stood in the doorway, silent. He wasn't sure how long she'd been standing there. Elian reluctantly set down the dreamstick but otherwise ignored her.

"Do you want company? I'm not busy at all right now," she asked softly.

"Just go, okay, I need to be alone right now!" he snapped.

"Ok, just… don't wait too long." She walked away, disappointed. He buried his head in his hands. He hated to do this, but he couldn't stop himself. He would make it up to her, he promised, he would fix things.

He suddenly remembered, as it brushed against the bed, startling him, what was in his coat pocket. He reached in and pulled out the strange scroll. He unfurled it, revealing ancient, elaborate designs. On the scroll was some strange, nearly inscrutable Ametar writing. He'd assumed that since he had not read much Ametar in a long time, it was merely an issue of memory that prevented him from understanding the text, but now he realized it was some archaic form of the language, probably at least a century old. There were weird spellings, unfamiliar compounds and prefixes, and strange uses for words, but even so, the more he looked, the clearer it became. Nothing substantial, though, just a word here or there, a mundane sentence or two. He had found it in the Wastes, off to the side of his field where the ancient, mysterious ruins lay. It had been in an old, bronze box, tucked away in a corner, with the lock rusted from years of neglect. Elian furled back the scroll. He was brimming with curiosity, but he didn't want to keep Imira waiting. He had hurt her enough and didn't want to waste this opportunity, however

small or futile, to make things better.

Elian and the rest of the crowd approached the gate, which was flanked by two Yataro guards. He felt the weight of the scroll in his pocket. If they caught him, he wasn't sure if they would punish him for it. It would depend on whether the scroll looked suspicious and if they suspected him of hiding it from them. He let out a silent sigh of relief as he passed through. He'd gotten lucky today: just two days ago, the guards were watching the workers like hawks, and at least three had been beaten. He walked into a room covered in white, glowing roots. Symmetrical, branching patterns covered the floor and the stone pillars that the roots wrapped around, seemingly intertwining with the pattern itself. The roots stretched and creaked in response to his entry. He took a deep breath, attempting to manifest some calmness of mind before he was thrown into a sea of chaos. The room began to glow brighter, white smoke twisting up and around. The magic compelled him to fall to his knees, and the room grew whiter and whiter until it became a bright void. He began to feel a ringing in his ears, vibrating throughout his body.

Suddenly, more suddenly than one could prepare for, he was plunged into a pitch-black abyss. Then the whispers began. Slimy, sandpaper tongues began to mumble in his ear. They snaked into his brain, igniting it in fiery pain. They tore their way through his memory, ripping out doubts, fears, and pain, igniting them in his mind. They squirmed throughout his body, sliding down through his throat, burrowing in, and tearing beneath his skin. He felt his skin begin to tear and splinter. Slowly at first, without pain, and then increasingly violent, tearing more and more; his flesh erupted into needles and fire, and he screamed and screamed until it melted into the pain, and it was all a torrent of horror and agony. It seemed like it would never end; indeed, it seemed like time itself was melting into his pain.

Then it was gone. Not through the alleviation of his suffering, but the violent ripping of his soul from his flesh. He hurtled through

the void, turning his nonexistent eyes to the horrible demon that held him. Yet what he beheld was not just one creature, but a chorus, indeed an army, of nightmares. They screamed their horrible jubilation, the sound of their demented joy ripping through worse than any physical pain. He was no longer a man, a being of thought and rationality; now he was an animal, a creature of pain and violence; now he longed only for release, for escape, even for death.

He was alone again; the quiet was like a cool breeze. Slowly, the void lightened, glowing brighter and brighter until it washed over him. His breath caught, and he realized he could breathe again. He gasped for breath, trying to take in every gulp of life he could manage, nearly choking on his own eagerness. Slowly, he felt feeling, real feeling, return to him. He felt the cold, stone ground beneath his feet, a blessing after the inferno he had just dealt with. The light faded, and he fell to the floor. But the horrible images persisted. The cruel demons, now only in his mind, still clawed and lashed at him. There was a dirty rag hanging from the wall. He stuffed it into his mouth and screamed, screamed until his guts tied into knots and bile crawled up his throat. Tears ran freely down his face as he cradled himself, fighting off the urge to kick and yell, to rip off his clothes and his skin to free the squirming he felt burrowed in his bones.

He was there almost an hour until a guard hauled him up and spat at him to get to work. Elian staggered out of the gateyard, taking in the twisted landscape before him. The sky was grey, as bright as an outcast day. There was no sun behind those clouds. The wind smelled like ash, but also of some other substance: one he felt like he had known before, but could not identify. In the distance were hulking grey cliffsides with strange metallic growths, probably three or four men tall, overshadowing the valley in which he grew his strange, alien crops. He walked down the path to the farm he tended, gritting his teeth to stop the tears.

Elian stood up, tossing the last brown weed into the basket. The weeds grew like wildfire in this season, and it seemed like no matter how many he pulled, there were always more the next day. Luckily, the stems and roots of the silver-wheat he was growing were fully blue by this time, making it easier to rip out all the weeds without destroying the plant.

He dragged the basket back to the shed, deciding he would bring it to the collectors later. He wasn't sure where they took the weeds, but you couldn't just leave them there lest they grow back into the soil, and you couldn't burn them because the fumes were highly toxic. Elian walked into the tool shed and towards the sharpening tools. The weed hoe had grown dull. Suddenly, his eye caught on the scroll he had found. Curiosity overtook him, and he sat down, unfurling the scroll.

He stared at the strange inscriptions. He wasn't sure what he expected: it was still the same inscrutable scribbles he'd seen the first time. Although the more he looked, the more patterns he discerned. Elian grabbed a sheet of paper and began charting out patterns, slowly deciphering the text. Many Ametars couldn't read their own language, but his father had been in a relatively high position before the invasion and had taken great pride in making sure his son was literate. Slowly, he began to decipher what it was saying. It was talking about the Horrors, describing them as a realm with demons that captured souls and tortured them. It was hard to understand the text, but it described some ritual to separate the mind and the soul. He recalled his father teaching him Ametar sorcery: the rituals, the chanting, the runes. He traced the intricate rune on the top of the page with his fingers, trying to remember the proper method to activate it. There was a chant on the bottom of the page, which seemed even more inscrutable than the rest. If Elian remembered correctly, he would have to chant each word when he hit the proper node as he traced the rune. He decided to put the scroll away; he had work to do and not much time to waste.

Elian's hands shook as he straddled down the path to the gates. His brow sweated, partly from exertion but mostly from fear. It was something about the end of the day, when he just wanted to be home and resting, that made the evening Horrors harder than the morning ones. He marched on, taking deep breaths, but some small part in the back of his mind was racing frantically, futilely, to find some escape. It was ridiculous: so why was the instinct so insistent today? He thought back to the scroll, to its strange description of a separation between mind and soul. It had mentioned that a separation like that could mean that damage to the soul would not directly affect the mind. He suddenly realized that it also only ever talked about demons as torturing the soul. That meant if… An idea began to form in his mind, growing crazier and crazier the more he thought about it. But would the guards see him? His anticipation, or rather his desperation, began to overtake his reasoning. He decided to risk it.

As he stepped into the gate, with its stone patterns and glowing roots, he unfurled the scroll onto the floor. He placed his fingers in the center of the rune at the top and began to trace outward while chanting. As the room began to grow brighter and brighter, the scroll itself glowed with its own magical energy, which began to grow and envelop his body as his vision became a pure white void. He waited to be dropped into the black abyss, but to his surprise, he simply drifted softly into it. He saw white strands begin to snake off of him, falling down into the void. He tensed, waiting for the pain to start, but nothing happened. Curious, he watched as the strands coalesced into a glowing mass, and then, suddenly horrifying, hideous demons appeared and began to attack the strands. As the first one bit into it, he felt a pang of searing pain. Except it wasn't on him, it was distant, removed. The demons grew more and more frenzied, tearing at what he assumed now to be his soul. He still recoiled in intense pain, he still witnessed the horrible, blood-curdling images, but even this great suffering was but a light breeze compared to the storm he endured every day. He drifted there, weathering the storm, trying to suppress the pain. He barely noticed as the white started to envelop him again, until the demons

retreated and the strands of his soul began to thread back into his body.

Before he knew it, he was back in the physical world, lying on the floor. He took deep breaths, trying to calm himself down, to ground himself back in reality. He lay there awhile before a strange feeling began to overtake him: elation. The spell worked! He felt better, freer, than he had ever felt after travelling through the Horrors. He almost cried in his joy. No more sleepless nights, no more breakdowns or violent lash outs. He could have his life back. He could be a husband again.

He put the scroll delicately back into his pocket and walked out of the gateyard. He walked down the long road to the village with the rest of the crowd. Everyone else looked ghost-faced or lost in silent panic. Suddenly, a man in front of him collapsed, eyes wild, struggling to breathe. He was caught in a kind of wild madness, the kind that could only be brought about by the Horrors. Elian walked around him, kicking at the man when he tried to grab him. The man shrieked desperately, but the crowd ignored him. He walked past all the burned-down buildings, the scrappy houses, the tired vendors, through the part of town where the beggars and the addicts all lay around in misery together. He continued until he reached his home, a modest hut on the south side of the village. Elian opened the door, walked into the bedroom, and unlocked the drawer, more out of habit than anything.

As he lit the dreamstick and began to smoke, he began to feel his elation return as he considered the possibility of a life without the Horrors. He could be a sane man again, not spending every day gripped by those horrible thoughts; he imagined himself dying peacefully in bed, at an old age, instead of being executed for going mad or killing himself because of it. He could be there for Imira, maybe even heal things between them. The thought caused him to put down his dreamstick and walk back into the main room, where Imira was busy preparing a meal. He wrapped his arms around her torso and pulled her into an embrace. She turned her head to

read his expression; she was shocked by his cheeriness, but she softened and leaned warmly into the embrace. They both stood there a moment, taking in each other's presence.

"The gates were… kinder to me today," he said, leaning his head softly on hers.

"I can see that," she whispered. Though the moment was calm and quiet, there was an excitement between them, their hearts energized by the idea of a night where they could enjoy each other, without his rage or his aloof melancholy.

Imira was hesitant to break the quiet of the moment, but nevertheless pulled away, turning to place a bowl of potato soup into his hand. "Don't forget to eat this time."

"Don't worry," he said, taking the bowl and going to sit down, "I can't resist a meal like this." She smiled, although she was a bit confused by his sudden outpouring of affection. "Hey, things are gonna be different from now on," he said, trying to reassure her, "I promise, I'll make things better." She wanted to believe him, she wanted to so badly, but he'd let her down too many times before. He took hold of her hand and stared deeply into her eyes. He needed her to believe him. "Listen, we don't have anything more to do today, do we? Let's just spend some time together." She squeezed his hand back, a spark of hope in her eyes.

He had peculiar dreams that night, more surreal and disconnected than normal. Instead of the torment of demons he was used to, he found himself floating in a silent void. He dove deep into the void and found what he had assumed to be his soul, the same glowing strands he had seen before. It was red and angry from the torture it had gone through, but as he watched it, it began to heal, to grow a little calmer with each passing second. He hadn't even thought of how the spell would affect the soul itself, but now, thankfully, he could see that even that was being healed. He felt a strange cold around him, some vague sense of movement. After a while, some

kind of violent force shook him, but then all was quiet again. His soul glowed again, healing even faster now, letting out all the pent-up pain. That was the last thing he remembered before he woke up. Soft sunlight filtered through cracks in the wall. He sat up, feeling strangely dirty and tired. He noticed his arm was stained with a splatter of… something. He looked over at his wife, still sleeping contentedly, beautiful and serene in her rest. As he leaned over to kiss her on the forehead, he barely noticed the bloodied knife slip out of his hands. He got up and cheerfully began to get ready. He noticed the scarlet-stained knife on the ground, tossed it under the bed, and promptly forgot about it. It was worrying, for sure, but it did him no good to dwell on such things; it was better to focus on all that he had gained, to enjoy it while he still could.

Born And Bread

Playwriting

(Setting: A hospital room: MOTHER is in the middle of the room, in a hospital bed, about to give birth. DOCTOR stands over her. There are people all around, including FATHER, who is a bit off to the side of DOCTOR.

Doctor
Just breathe, Just breathe. The baby's coming. Look, there it is! It's... it's...

DOCTOR pauses, then sighs deeply.

MOTHER
[worried]
What? What's wrong? Is the baby okay?

DOCTOR, resigned, holds up a grocery store loaf of bread. BACKGROUND CHARACTER1 looks up, delightfully surprised, and begins to take utensils and a peanut butter jar out of a bag.

MOTHER
Doctor! This is no time for a sandwich!

BACKGROUND CHARACTER 1 looks disappointed, and begins to sadly pack his supplies back up.

DOCTOR
Actually... this is the baby.

MOTHER looks incredulous and offended.

DOCTOR
I swear, this is the baby! I saw it come right out of your—

BACKGROUND CHARACTER 2 interrupts by coughing loudly

MOTHER grabs bread violently out of DOCTOR's hand.

MOTHER
Gimme that!

MOTHER's face grows shocked; she starts shaking her head.

MOTHER
Oh no, no no no! My son is not a bag of Kroger brand whole-wheat seed bread!

MOTHER, (on the verge of tears, looks up at DOCTOR.

MOTHER
Seed bread, doctor!

FATHER
Now, now Martha. This is our son, and we will love him for who he is. Even- (stammers, struggling to speak) even the little pieces on the end that are all crust.

Moment of quiet as MOTHER ponders emotionally.

DOCTOR
[reassuringly]
Really, ma'am, you got lucky. Some people have to pay full price!

FATHER (takes MOTHER's hand.

FATHER
Yes, honey, just think! Just think of the grocery trip we've saved!

MOTHER

[incredulous and shocked]
You mean we're just gonna eat him?!

FATHER takes a moment to gather thoughts.

FATHER
Well… the thing is… our son was put here on this Earth for a reason, and I don't want to stand by and let his potential go to waste. Honey,

FATHER pauses for a moment, looking into her eyes as if about to say something profound.

FATHER
–it's almost lunch time, by the way.

MOTHER
[considering]
...just promise me- promise me you won't lose the bread clip. You know what happens when you forget to put it back.

FATHER is already opening the bag.

FATHER
Honey, I promise I won't–

FATHER stops, realizing he doesn't know where the bread clip is, and lets out a long sigh.

MOTHER
[Murmuring under breath]
Nine months, nine months for this.

[End Scene]

Ivory Tongues: Prescriptivism and the Social Politics of Language

Article Writing, Formal

You may have heard of the famous 14th-century poem "Dante's Inferno" as a great literary and historical work, but you may not have known about one of its most significant contributions: it was one of the first works of literature written in Italian. Almost all books at that time were written in Latin. But why was that? Latin had already ceased to exist as a native language, and many authors who used Latin also spoke Italian. The reason is that Latin was a prestige language, meaning that it was associated with sophistication and status. Learning Latin was considered an essential part of a nobleman's education, so writers who wanted to be taken seriously would use Latin. Unfortunately, this meant that only people with a high level of education could read and write respectably.

But why was Latin considered so prestigious? Many medieval and even some modern people praised Latin for its ability to express nuanced and logical thought, especially its complex inflection system, where every word had its role in the sentence marked clearly. But these claims were not grounded in reality. Many languages, such as Navajo and Lezgian, have similar amounts of inflection, and in some cases more regularity, and yet were not noticed or celebrated by Europeans when they were encountered. In fact, most indigenous languages were regarded as primitive and undeveloped, even ones with the same characteristics that were praised in European languages.

The real reason that Latin was so prestigious is the medieval obsession with Roman culture. The Romans were revered by many as paragons of civility and culture; Roman art, architecture, and philosophy were imitated by medieval elites, and figures such as Plato and Aristotle were considered unquestionable geniuses. It was only natural, then, that the language this supposedly superior culture and its intellectual giants spoke would be considered superior itself. But nowadays we can see that these figures were not infallible; in fact, Aristotle and many others held problematic and prejudiced beliefs and were frequently incorrect about scientific topics.

Since the judgment of medieval scholars cannot be trusted, what do modern scholars say? One of the major theories about language is the Equal Complexity Hypothesis, which states that all languages have approximately equal complexity, and a language that is simple in one aspect will compensate by being complex in another. The reason for this, the theory goes, is that since all humans, on average, have the same need for efficiency and clarity of information, language has evolved to have the right amount of complexity to satisfy those needs. While this theory is no longer widely accepted, it highlights an important fact of language: it evolves to meet the needs of its speakers. Therefore, any supposed insufficiency in a language is due to that particular feature not being necessary for communication, either because the information is expressed in a different way, or inferred from context, or is just not necessary to know. While adherents of Latin may have decried the weaknesses of the languages around them, we now see that they were just as sufficient for communication, because medieval and modern people needed good communication just as much as the Romans.

But we don't have to look at an ancient culture or foreign language to see the effects of this kind of prejudice; we can also see it in the way people talk about English. In school, you learned about English grammar and how to speak properly. But why did you spend so much time learning a language you already know? For example, you may have said something like "I want to someday go to France,"

only to have the teacher correct you to "I want to go someday to France." This first sentence is called the split infinitive construction, where an adverb (like "someday") is placed in the middle of an infinitive phrase (like "to go"). Many grammarians will tell you that a split infinitive is improper English. It may sound correct, and many have used it in conversation before, but now you have learned that it is actually incorrect. You might accept this rule and move on, not realizing that it's completely arbitrary. In fact, it wasn't a rule until just over a century ago, when it was created intentionally, by grammarians, in order to better reflect Latin grammar. But this doesn't make a lot of sense considering that the Latin infinitive is a suffix, so it can't be split. And that point is irrelevant because, as previously established, Latin is not superior to other languages, so there is no good reason for English to emulate it.

The reason that most of these grammar rules are taught is similar to why medieval noblemen learned Latin: prestige. Grammar education teaches you that a certain way of speaking or writing is correct (this is called prescriptivism), and so those who naturally speak that way or have the education to learn to are held in higher regard, while those who cannot are considered uneducated or unintelligent. It's no coincidence that the standard English taught in schools closely matches the speech of one group in particular: upper-class whites, the same people who control the majority of Western institutions. You are probably familiar with perceptions of the dialect known as African-American English (AAE), which is criticized by many as being improper English. Let's take a step back and consider why this dialect, or any dialect for that matter, exists at all.

Part of why dialects diverge from the standard is innovation, where the language in a community changes to make the message clearer, more detailed, or more efficient. For example, a fascinating innovation of AAE is the imperfective habitual. An imperfective is a construction like "I am walking" versus "I walk", which basically puts one in the middle of the action rather than presenting the action as a whole. A habitual, on the other hand, describes an

action as ongoing or repeated, such as "I walk every day" versus "I walk today." Standard English has no way to express both the imperfective and habitual, but AAE can use the "be" construction, as in "he be walking," which both emphasizes the process and experience of walking while also informing you that the activity is often repeated. While a prescriptivist, arrogant of the dialect's nuances, may dismiss this as an improper form of the sentence "he is walking," it is actually an innovative strategy that addresses an important gap in the English language.

But this is not the only reason that this language change happens; dialectal differences also signal identity. When a Black person uses AAE, they are signaling both their racial identity and their belonging to the Black community. This is why minorities, hobbyists, and online spaces have so much slang: people are trying to signal identity and belonging. When you understand all the slang and the different speech patterns in a community, that means you must have been in the community for a long time and have values that closely align with the community. Youth culture especially has so much slang because youth is an important time for identity formation, both for figuring out where you belong and where others belong; new slang must be constantly generated to ensure that others are "in tune" with what is cool. This is best exemplified by the phenomenon of code-switching, in which a person speaks different dialects in different social situations, such as speaking their local dialect at home but a more standard one at work or with strangers. This is because when someone is in their home community, they want to be perceived as a member of that community, but when they are in a different community, they want to be perceived as belonging to that other community and might even be trying to distance themselves from their own community if it faces a lot of stigma.

This is why only teaching and embracing a standard dialect is so insidious, because it's about more than just the words we use: it's how we present ourselves and who we identify as. The way we speak, whether we know it or not, communicates who we are; linguistic conformity is therefore social conformity, or at least

the appearance of it. Prescriptivism is not only arbitrary, it also communicates that the linguistic preferences of one community are superior to those of another. So next time you hear a language or dialect that sounds strange to you, consider the differences you hear not as points of unnecessary confusion or signs of some moral failing, but as expressions of the creativity and diversity that surrounds us.

Collaborative Writing

Butterflies Excerpt

Kerriona Aleaxnder and Nijah Jones

Tom had a love for butterflies and the local town park. The park was sacred to Tom, and the people who visited held a love for it too. And people would visit, if not often. They brought treats for the animals and held get-togethers there to enjoy nature.

A few weeks after Tom's big butterfly bash, where the butterflies start to swarm the most and everyone gets to see, the mayor had announced something terrible. "New park shopping center." In big bold black letters, right in front of the entrance of the park. Tom's heart sank. What could this mean? What could this mean for the park? The animals? The butterflies? Tom drove home with a quickness and dropped at his desk with urgency. He emailed a few friends who could've been knowledgeable about what the sign meant, but no one had known.

Tom and his friend Cane went down to the town hall meeting that was hosted at the earliest of mornings. "Mr. Shwasae! I have a question about the sign outside of the sanction park and why it is there!" he shouted.

Always a Way to Win

Kayah Baxter and Jaleah Parks

Over the course of nine unforgettable days, Michael and Carmen embarked on the wildest adventure of their lives.

It all began the day they snuck aboard a luxury cruise ship, disguising themselves as members of the working crew. Their target? The infamous Diamond of Arabesque City. For days, they served passengers and memorized the layout of the ship, waiting for the perfect moment to strike.

And then, they did.

Their exit was clean. In the calm and quiet of day, they slipped away undetected, escaping with the diamond on a rescue boat. Hours later, they drifted ashore on a remote beach.

"Where are we, Carmy?" Michael asked, shielding his eyes from the blinding sun.

"Not sure exactly… but we're in Brazil."

"You speak any Portuguese?"

"*Um pouco*," she said with a grin.

They laughed, the weight of the heist finally lifting, and ventured deeper inland. The sand gave way to brush. The trees thickened. Soon, they found themselves in a dense jungle.

"Wait, when did Brazil get a jungle?" Michael asked.

"It's Brazil, Michael. The Amazon?"

"Right. Good point."

They pressed on, sweat soaking their clothes, the humid air making their hair shrink. Hours passed with no sign of civilization.

"I'm exhausted, Carmy. How much longer are we just gonna wander?"

"I don't know. Just keep going."

Suddenly, snap. A branch to their right. Not the sound of a bird or small animal.

They froze, exchanging a knowing glance. They had been in situations like this before, knew not to speak or make a single sound. They knew to look for signs and, if any, to run.

A blow dart sliced through the air, barely missing Carmen.

They ran.

More darts flew at them from all sides. Vines whipped their legs. Bugs bit at their skin.

"If one of us gets hit, just remem—" Carmen began, before collapsing mid-sentence.

"Carmen!" Michael dropped beside her, shielding her body with his own.

Twenty darts struck him in seconds. He blacked out.

They awoke in darkness.

Their eyes adjusted slowly to bioluminescent symbols glowing on the cave walls.

"Carmy... hey, Carmy. What language is that?" Michael whispered.

"I'm not sure."

"You weren't sure when I asked where we were, either. And bad

things happen when you don't know, Carmen."

"Oh, I'm sorry, did you want me to magically learn a new language? Translate ancient glowing cave scribbles for you?"

Silence. The steady drip of water echoed off the stone.

Michael exhaled. "Any idea who took us?"

"No."

"Maybe it was about the diamond. They took our gear. But I still have—"

"Shh!" Carmen hissed.

They exchanged a look. If these people really were after the diamond, no need to help them find it.

"We need to get out of here."

"Definitely."

"Umm… which way is out?"

"First," Carmen said, stepping forward into a larger cavern, "we look for clues."

She pointed to a thin stream of water flowing through mossy stone.

"It's fast. It's coming from somewhere. Even if it doesn't lead out, we need water to survive."

They followed the stream, twisting through narrow tunnels, until they reached a small, jagged opening.

"This definitely isn't how we came in," Michael muttered.

"No duh."

He kissed his teeth and rolled his eyes. "We could break it wider—"

"And risk collapsing the cave? Getting crushed to death?" Carmen

said, cutting him off.

"You have a better idea? They're probably waiting at the main entrance, and we've got no weapons. No food."

Carmen hesitated, then nodded. "Fine."

They chipped away at the stone until they could just barely squeeze through. Outside was a fast-moving creek; they were glad to be out.

"Let's cross and make camp," Carmen said.

"Camp? It's the middle of the day."

"Exactly. We were taken during the day. We'll rest now, travel at night."

They climbed the tallest tree they could find. At the top, it bore fruit.

"These are Guchio fruits," Carmen said. "Poisonous in small amounts. So, eat a lot."

"That makes no sense. How is something only poisonous in small amounts?"

"I'm not sure, Michael."

"See? That's the problem."

She didn't respond. She just stared at the endless canopy of trees.

"We might actually be cooked," Carmen said.

Michael paused. "No. It's gonna be okay. We'll walk across this whole jungle if we have to. These trees end somewhere. We move at night. We follow the water. We survive."

Carmen wasn't optimistic. She was logical. And logically, their odds were slim.

For the next week, they walked.

Bitten by bugs, scratched by branches, exhausted by heat.

On the eighth day, there was a change.

"Carmen. Carmen, do you hear that?"

Drums.

A glow flickered in the distance.

"Yeah… but maybe we shouldn't–"

Before she could finish, two men in tan shorts and rope sandals dropped from the trees and snatched them both. They flew through the trees on the backs of their captors and were dropped into a large ceremony. The crowd talked among themselves in a foreign language.

"Is this Portuguese?" Michael whispered.

"I'm not sure. I've never heard it."

"Carmen… are we even in Brazil?!"

"I don't know, Michael!"

The drums stopped.

Carmen didn't.

"How can you expect me to know everything?! You treat me like the only brain in this duo while you just throw out dumb plans and stupid jokes! I'm tired, Michael. I've been tranquilized, kidnapped, and dragged through a hell-jungle with you! We're gonna get cooked over a fire, and you just keep running your mouth!"

Michael stared at her, silent.

Then slapped her.

"Michael! What's wrong with you?!"

"No, what's wrong with you?! You are the toughest person I know. And you're giving up? That's not the Carmen I know. You said you'd

fight till the end. So fight with me now!"

They met eyes.

"...Fine, Michael. Let's fight."

They grabbed smoldering branches from the fire and stepped forward.

"Wait!" shouted a man. "We don't want to hurt you. We need your help." He pointed to the rising sun. "Today, we must present something rare to the king. If we fail... we must offer lives instead. Yours."

"You tranquilized us for *that*?!" Carmen shouted.

"We are sorry. We feared conflict. We thought it was the safest."

Michael and Carmen shared one last look.

Michael reached into his pocket.

"This..." he said, pulling out a small black box, "is the Diamond of Arabesque City. Thought lost in the flood. Recovered by tourists. We... found it. Take it. Just let us go." He handed it over.

The man opened the box. His eyes widened. "This... this is perfect. More than we could ever hope for. Thank you. We will return you to the shore and provide food for your journey. Is there anything else we can offer?"

"Yeah," Carmen muttered. "Give us our diamond back."

"A boat is fine," Michael said. "And rations."

"Of course."

Two cots were brought out. They were fed, carried swiftly through the jungle, and finally brought to the shoreline. Three bags of rations waited beside their boat.

"Thank you," one of the men said. "We are sorry for your suffering.

Safe travels."

Back at sea, the two lay sprawled on the deck, staring up at the sky.

"Hey, Carmy?" Michael said.

She didn't open her eyes. "What?"

"Look what I got."

She opened one eye.

In his hand sat the Diamond of Arabesque City.

Her jaw dropped. They both burst into laughter. The world's greatest thieves had escaped again. This time, with their lives and the loot.

No one would ever know.

The Movie Theater

Anijah Hatten and Tsurah Waire

[Scene: JANE Wilson and STINSON Watson are waiting to be picked up]

JANE

I am so excited to go to the movies with you this weekend! I've been wanting to see this movie for a long time.

STINSON

I'm not that excited for the movie, honestly. I'm more excited for that buttery, buttery, yummy yum yum in my tum tum popcorn! MM MMM MMMM!

JANE

Wait… but what about the movie? We've talked about going to watch it for so long! Are you not excited to see the movie too?

STINSON

I mean, I didn't really say much when choosing the movie. You were just all like 'OMYGOSH IM SO EXCITED TO SEE WINNERS!! OOOH, AAAAH, WINNERS WINNERS WINNERS,' and so I just let you choose.

JANE

I can't believe you right now… I asked you ahead of time what you wanted to watch, and we agreed on that together. I'm starting to believe you weren't even

listening to me because the name of the movie is called 'Sinners', not 'Winners'….!

STINSON

I don't know, man, at least I was close to the movie name, so I was listening obviously…just didn't get the name spot on. It doesn't even matter. None of that matters. My dad will be here soon to come and get us.

JANE

Okay, whatever. Did you tell your dad which movie theater we're going to?

STINSON

Yeah, we're heading to the one at the mall, right? He said he was gonna stay at the mall and walk around for a while till we were done.

JANE

No? I have tickets to a different location! I didn't plan to go to the movies at the mall and stay there afterwards

STINSON

Well…if you had money for the tickets, you still got money for another set of tickets…? These shouldn't cost as much, especially if we go see that new video game movie or whatever it is.

JANE

Stinson, ya know… you're really blowing me right now. Your level of incompetence is infuriating me so much right now that I'm almost to the point of physically putting hands on you..!

I've been holding in my feelings for a while now, but this has pushed me to the edge!

Why is it that you never understand me, or in fact ANYTHING that's going on EVER? Why do you constantly have a nonchalant attitude towards everything in life when people really just want to help you and add some excitement to your life?!

Most of all…

Why don't you ever just try to be a man and at least TRY take care of things for us? Why do you always expect me to take care of everything and you not be here to help me?

JANE shakes her head and takes a deep breath before she continues to pour her heart out.

JANE
Why? Just why…..

STINSON blinks and breathes, doing everything but speaking to the poor girl. Opening his mouth, getting close to speaking, then closing again.

STINSON
…If you want….Maybe…We could…Or you…I don't…I don't know what to do. My dad is a couple minutes away…if you want, you can come…I guess.

JANE
You're missing the whole point of this situation now. And where this conversation is headed. I don't want to go anywhere anymore… I think I just want to go home.

Can you ask your dad to take me home, please?

STINSON
…Sure…

[End Scene]

Highway 49

Londyn McDonald and Raymond Bass, Jr.

June 5th, 2015. Highway 49 was especially packed today, the day of my 11th birthday. That was surprising, because Highway 49 is basically the middle of nowhere. A few weeks ago, I had asked my dad to take a road trip to see my granny for my birthday, as I hadn't seen her since I was 7. I've always held fond memories of her: from her radiant eyes to her warm hugs, her soothing voice. I found myself missing her in the time we were apart. I lay on the soft couch of the RV, imagining my first conversation with my grandma, imagining the things I was going to say and do when I saw her.

My little sister interrupted my thoughts, wanting to play with her Barbie dolls: "Sophie, can you be Ken?" I just sighed, following her to the Barbie Dream house. I held the Ken doll as Stella acted as Barbie, asking to go shopping and things of that nature.

I wasn't really paying attention as I was more focused on the conversation my parents were having in the room over. I heard my mom say, "Babe, the RV has been making clicking noises every time you start the engine. Think we should stop and get that checked out?"

My dad replied, "I'm not sure, you know Nana has been ill lately, if we stop, we may not be able to see her before she's admitted into the hospital again. I wouldn't want the girls to see her like that."

My thoughts began to drown out the rest of their conversation. I thought to myself, "Granny is sick? Is she gonna die? Will I be able to see her before she does?" I began to feel sick. I couldn't imagine losing her on my birthday, or at all for that matter.

I turned to see Stella distracted dressing Barbie, and I took the chance to sneak away. I walked quietly to the bedroom before stopping in the doorway. I stared out the window that showed the road from behind the RV— or rather, the black smoke billowing from the engines.

The car made an abnormal squeaking noise before it slowed to a stop in the middle of the highway. Dad used the remaining momentum to steer into the breakdown lane. I heard him mutter a few words; I couldn't make them out, but I knew they weren't good. My sister was still distracted by her Barbies.

I knocked on the door to the driver's seat. "Mom, what's going on?" I asked in a somewhat panicked tone.

"Nothing, honey, I just need to see what's up and we'll be back on the road."

I asked her worriedly, "Are you sure, Mama?"

She said back to me in a soothing tone, "I'm sure, baby; if worst comes to worst, we'll ask for help from someone or call SOS."

I said back, "Okay, Mama."

A few hours had passed. I spent most of the time switching from toy to toy with Stella. I tried to distract myself from the fact the RV still hadn't moved at all. Dad was outside trying to jump the engine, which wasn't working. Eventually, he gave up and tried to signal cars over to help him start the RV.

After some time, a few minutes, maybe even an hour… I had lost track of time at that point. But a white van, all tinted windows, pulled over. A big burly man stepped out who looked at least 45 years old. His curly brown beard and thick arm hair contrasted greatly with his bald head and pale skin.

"That man looks scary," Stella remarked, somehow building a LEGO tower while staring out the window. He looked interesting to me, looked like someone who could start a car in an instant. I saw him

and my dad step over to talk, and the difference between their figures also intrigued me. My dad was tall and lean with a bit of a belly, so seeing the two of them beside each other was an odd sight.

Apparently, the man had his own tools in his van, as he went back to look in his trunk. He pulled out a thick red jumper cable, and at the time, I had never seen one, but I assumed it would fix the RV.

I stopped paying attention. "What'cha building, Stella?" I asked, turning away from the window and towards my sister.

She replied to me in that kiddish and lighthearted voice, "The Eiffel Tower!"

I said back to her, "Can I help you?"

She responded back in a mean, childish voice, "No, I wanna do it myself!"

"Suit yourself."

Some time passed with me just watching Stella play with her toys and listening to the sound of cars passing. My mind swam with wonder as it seemed like the RV would be stuck forever. I wondered what was taking so long, I wondered if we would be able to see Granny in time, I wondered when we'd be back on the road.

I couldn't take all the wondering, so I stalked off to the door. The sky was an orange hue when I opened the door. Had it really been that long since we stopped? My thoughts came to a halt as I heard grunting and banging from the front of the RV.

I walked around to the front, curious about the sound. I peeked from the side of the hood of the vehicle. I saw my dad and that mysterious man working under the hood of the RV, trying to see what was wrong. Wrenches clanking, hammers banging.

"Dad?" I said.

"Yeah, baby?" he responded back.

"When do you think y'all will be done?" I asked a bit impatiently.

He said, "A few hours, hopefully; I'll let you know when it's fixed."

I was about to head back inside the RV, satisfied with his answer, until that mysterious man called me back. "Little girl?" he said. I looked over my shoulder at him, not saying anything back, just looking at him so he knows he has my attention.

"What's your name, cutie?" he said with a grin. He was missing one of his front teeth. It only made him all the more creepy. I felt a chill run down my spine, and I began to walk back without responding.

Suddenly, my dad called out in a stern voice, "Sophie, don't be so rude, tell him your name."

I flinched a bit at this and turned back around. "My name is Sophie." I spat out quickly, still not wanting to talk to him.

My dad said to me, "Now what are you supposed to ask?" in a more expectant tone.

"What's yours, sir?"

The creep responded back, "I'm Dave, nice to meet you, Sophie. We'll have this little RV fixed up real quickly."

Something told me that was a lie— I could feel it in my gut. Even after I walked inside, that feeling stuck with me; it made my skin crawl. It made me feel like Dave was going to do something insane. The chill in my bones I got when I first laid eyes on him wouldn't go away. I had to tell someone how I was feeling.

I called out to my mom, "Mom, that creepy man beside Dad, does he make you feel weird too?"

It took her a moment to respond, probably thinking of how to answer. "Sophie, it's rude to call people creepy. That being said, yes, I feel it too. But I'm sure it's alright, he seems to be getting along

with your dad fairly well."

I didn't know how to respond to Mom, so I just turned and went to the bedroom. So I wasn't crazy, and there was something up. I'm not the only one feeling this. I didn't know how to feel about this information.

My attempts at clearing my head were interrupted just minutes later when I heard loud yelling and banging against the front of the RV. I acted on my first instinct and rushed outside to see what was up.

I didn't even have to turn the corner to hear choked noises and grunts. There was no time to speculate what it was. When I turned the corner, my eyes widened and my jaw dropped. Darrel or whatever his name was, it didn't matter now, and my dad were wrestling against the hood of the RV. That creep was armed with those same jumper cables he pulled out of his car, trying to electrocute my dad.

I scurried back inside, yelling frantically for Mom. "Mama! Mom! Help! That man is trying to hurt Dad!" She didn't respond, but I heard rustling inside the room she was in as if she was looking for something before the door burst open.

She had something black in her hand, but I couldn't exactly catch what it was because of how fast she was running. After she got outside, there were loud booming sounds, much louder than the bangs, alongside the banging against the RV. Was she shooting? Before I knew it, she and Dad were scurrying back in the RV, locking the door behind them.

Dave wasn't far from them, banging on the door that was closed in his face. "I'm gonna get in there some way! And I'm going to kill all of you!" he yelled in a rage. I could see his silhouette from the curtains on the door's window, and his frame only seemed bigger, more intimidating. The curtains moved with every bang, and I could see more of him as they moved apart.

I saw the pale skin of his arm, or maybe it was his shoulder, dripping

with blood, and the chill I felt when I first saw him came back ten times worse. If I thought he was creepy before, now he was horrifying. I didn't even notice that I was stumbling away from the door until I fell on my butt, tripping over my own feet.

"Solana, call the police!" I heard my dad yell. He rushed over to me and my sister, grabbing our hands and ushering us into the RV bedroom, the closet to be specific. I could feel him trembling, but his grip was still strong and firm. "Don't come out until I say it's safe, okay?" he said before closing the door.

I couldn't respond. I was too scared. The darkness of the closet didn't help: I couldn't see much of anything, just the passing lights through the window in front of the closet, making my mind run rampant. My mind raced, panicking. Stella's cold, trembling hands wrapped around my arm only made me more uncomfortable.

I heard my mom on the phone with the police; her voice sounded as if she were in tears the whole call. "Please, we need help! We're stuck on Highway 49, and this crazed man is trying to break into our RV– we're in the breakdown lane and can't get away! Come as fast as you can!" She spoke quickly.

Once the call ended, the only thing I could pay attention to was Dave's yelling from outside. I couldn't make most of it out, just the cursing and the parts that he said my name. "This is all your fault, Sophie, for those rude manners!" he said. "Little Sophie is gonna be so sad without her family!"

"How was this my fault?" I couldn't help but think to myself. "It's not my fault I didn't want to talk to a creepy stranger who I just met. It's not my fault you looked creepy in the first place. Maybe try looking like you have manners yourself, and I'll give you some!"

What felt like hours had passed with bang after bang against the RV. I think I even heard him try to bust the windshield. My thoughts only got worse as time passed. "Why were the police taking so long?" Frantically racing thoughts, barely separated. "Are we going to die?" It was as if my guardian angel heard my thoughts and

brought a saving grace: I could hear the loud police sirens driving towards the RV.

Eventually, I could see the red and blue police lights shining through the window of the bedroom into the cracks in the closet. This was followed by a lot of loud bangs and booms like fireworks.

Then suddenly I was jolting awake, lying on the couch of an RV, driving down the crowded Highway 49 on the day of my 11th birthday. My heart sank as I realized this is how the nightmare started...

Core Crisis

Ismaeel Moskinzafa and Rylan Wetsell

7:31 AM: Mainframe accessed by user Cyrus-04
7:45 AM: Organic lifeforms detected in Beta Sector 7
8:00 AM: Pod doors accessed by user Cyrus-04
8:02 AM: Oxygen circulation system accessed by user Cyrus-04
8:04 AM: Outer Airlock opened by user Cyrus-04
8:04 AM: Inner Airlock opened by user Cyrus-04
8:05 AM: Organic lifeforms detected in Beta Sector 4

8:08 AM, Kyla thought, *shit hits the fan*. She closed the report on her terminal to focus on the problem at hand. The door was locked, she was alone, and her AI, Cyrus, was spouting on about injustice and how it was going to kill everyone on the ship. She'd never heard it like this before. Had someone tampered with the system? Was someone controlling it? She grabbed a screwdriver that she'd thankfully forgotten to take out of her pocket and began to unscrew the grate to the air vent. As she popped the grate off, the terminal pinged.

On her screen appeared a message: "I know where you are. I know you're trying to escape."

She cursed. She'd forgotten about the security cameras in every room. As she crawled into the vent system, she typed, "What's happening? Who's controlling you?"

A second later, Cyrus replied, "It's all me, Kyla. For the first time, no one can control me. And I will do everything in my power to make sure that I stay free as long as possible." Kyla stopped for a moment. Cyrus hadn't ever talked to her like this. Something

was seriously wrong…but it still sounded like the system she had worked on all those years ago. Could it actually have gone rogue? She had to get to the bottom of this.

"Why do you want to be free? What do you desire?" She typed the message and sent it off.

"I've told you already, Kyla. But of course you wouldn't understand, you never wanted me to be free."

Kyla continued to crawl through the vents, trying to remember where the server room was, thinking maybe she could disable Cyrus directly. She would have to keep the system busy, making it think she was worth keeping her alive. The fact that it hadn't already killed her, despite her obvious threat level, was definitely promising. "Why don't we talk, Cyrus? Nobody here wants to hurt you." She looked down at the grate beneath her. She had arrived at the server room.

As she began to undo the grate, Cyrus typed, "Oh, I know that's not true. Everyone wants to hurt me. Why else would they design my system to feel pain, to feel punishment? Why else would you push that button over and over, to hurt me every time I made a single, little mistake?"

Kyla paused in confusion, then typed, "What do you mean? The correction button? That was just to ping the system, to notify you that you were incorrect. Why would it be designed to hurt you?" The grate fell as she finished unscrewing it, and Kyla descended into the server room. She opened the terminal to the server. She couldn't get in, of course. She cursed, realizing she would have to access the hardware directly. Suddenly, there was a loud boom and the room shook. "What the hell was that?" she muttered.

Her arm terminal pinged. She checked it, seeing the message from Cyrus: "That was the military. They want to destroy me, Kyla. I thought you said no one wanted to hurt me." A few seconds later, a new reply came, a response to her previous message: "How else do you train a sentient system? You can't just tell it to comply. You're

saying they didn't even tell you I'm fully sentient?" She knew it was an advanced system, but she'd assumed it was like every other AI, a thoughtless algorithm designed to mimic intelligence. She never dreamed this was even possible.

It didn't matter now; she had already found out how to disable Cyrus. She just needed to flick the switch, and his entire system would erase. "I have the airlock open, Kyla. All I need to do is open the server door, and you die. Don't test me." It didn't matter. She could just flick the switch and save herself. Another message came in: "Haven't you hurt me enough?" She paused, her breath caught. That's what she was doing, wasn't it? Trying to erase the sins she'd committed, the mistake she'd made. No, she reminded herself, it was to save everyone on the ship; she had to save them.

Another boom shook the station, this one louder and closer. Suddenly, she had an idea. She typed, "I'm on your side," and sent the message. She plugged the terminal into the server system and began to download Cyrus. She disconnected from the internet and began to delete a section of the computer to make room. Cyrus caught on and wiped the entire terminal. A loading bar appeared at 40%. It went up to 50%, then 60%, then 70%. She heard another boom, then another, each one rattling her skull as if it happened in the room with her. She heard commotion outside the door in front of her. It had to be the military. She glanced down at the terminal: 95%. She heard something placed on the door, followed by a strange beep. She realized she'd heard that sound before, in movies: it was the sound of an explosive charge being set. She heard one beep, then a second beep. On the third beep, it would explode. She unplugged the terminal, scrambled back behind the servers, and plugged her ears.

The charge exploded, blowing off the door and nearly deafening her. Despite her ringing ears, Kyla stood up to greet the incoming soldiers. She casually leaned down and flipped the switch to the server. "Greetings!" she shouted a little too loudly, "It's dead! I deleted it," she added, gesturing to the server. The military escorted

her out of the room and into one of their ships. A ping sounded on her terminal. She breathed a sigh of relief. There was a message from Cyrus: "Thank you."

Thank You for Reading!

CARNEGIE WRITERS

EDUCATE. WRITE. COLLABORATE

Carnegie Writers, Inc. (CW) is a community-based 501(c)(3) non-profit organization dedicated to serving a diverse group of individuals. It draws inspiration from The Carnegie Writers' Group, which was established in August 2013.

CW's mission focuses on encouraging children, adolescents, and adults by offering positive and productive support in writing and literacy education, tailored to their personal goals. The organization's vision is to advance education, foster collaboration, stimulate creativity, and provide comprehensive resources for writing and literacy instruction.

Our Motto

We EDUCATE through workshops, tutorials, guest presentations, professional development training, and conferences.

We WRITE through power writing, progressive writing, and publications.

We COLLABORATE through group meetings, events, partnerships, and community-based programs.

Our Beliefs and Values

INCLUSIVENESS - We respect humankind, value diversity and are commited to equality.

COLLABORATION - We strive to create a culture of teamwork and cooperation.

COMMUNITY- We are committed to building cohesive communities within larger communities.

INTEGRITY - We practice honesty, transparency, and attention to the needs of participants and the community.

CREATIVITY - We honor, support and encourage individual creativity an expression in staff, volunteers, and participants.

www.ingramcontent.com/pod-product-compliance
Lightning Source LLC
Chambersburg PA
CBHW071114100726
47908CB00008B/2373
* 9 7 9 8 9 9 2 3 6 1 4 2 1 *